Rethinking Economi
Social Justice

The dominant approach to economic policy has so far failed to adequately address the pressing challenges the world faces today: extreme poverty, widespread joblessness and precarious employment, burgeoning inequality, and large-scale environmental threats. This message was brought home forcibly by the 2008 global economic crisis.

Rethinking Economic Policy for Social Justice shows how human rights have the potential to transform economic thinking and policy-making with far-reaching consequences for social justice. The authors make the case for a new normative and analytical framework, based on a broader range of objectives which have the potential to increase the substantive freedoms and choices people enjoy in the course of their lives and not upon narrow goals such as the growth of gross domestic product. The book covers a range of issues including inequality, fiscal and monetary policy, international development assistance, financial markets, globalization, and economic instability. This new approach allows for a complex interaction between individual rights, collective rights, and collective action, as well as encompassing a legal framework which offers formal mechanisms through which unjust policy can be protested.

This highly original and accessible book will be essential reading for human rights advocates, economists, policy-makers, and those working on questions of social justice.

Radhika Balakrishnan is the Faculty Director at the Center for Women's Global Leadership, and Professor of Women's and Gender Studies at Rutgers University, USA.

James Heintz is the Andrew Glyn Professor of Economics and Associate Director of the Political Economy Research Institute at the University of Massachusetts Amherst, USA.

Diane Elson is Emeritus Professor of Sociology at the University of Essex, Visiting Professor at the Centre for Research on Women in Scotland's Economy at Glasgow Caledonian University, and Research Associate of the Center for Women's Global Leadership at Rutgers University, USA.

Economics as Social Theory
Series edited by Tony Lawson
University of Cambridge

Social Theory is experiencing something of a revival within economics. Critical analyses of the particular nature of the subject matter of social studies and of the types of method, categories and modes of explanation that can legitimately be endorsed for the scientific study of social objects, are re-emerging. Economists are again addressing such issues as the relationship between agency and structure, between economy and the rest of society, and between the enquirer and the object of enquiry. There is a renewed interest in elaborating basic categories such as causation, competition, culture, discrimination, evolution, money, need, order, organization, power probability, process, rationality, technology, time, truth, uncertainty, value, etc.

The objective for this series is to facilitate this revival further. In contemporary economics the label "theory" has been appropriated by a group that confines itself to largely asocial, ahistorical, mathematical "modelling". Economics as Social Theory thus reclaims the "Theory" label, offering a platform for alternative rigorous, but broader and more critical conceptions of theorizing.

Other titles in this series include:

1. Economics and Language
Edited by Willie Henderson

2. Rationality, Institutions and Economic Methodology
Edited by Uskali Mäki, Bo Gustafsson, and Christian Knudsen

3. New Directions in Economic Methodology
Edited by Roger Backhouse

4. Who Pays for the Kids?
Nancy Folbre

5. Rules and Choice in Economics
Viktor Vanberg

6. Beyond Rhetoric and Realism in Economics
Thomas A. Boylan and Paschal F. O'Gorman

7. Feminism, Objectivity and Economics
Julie A. Nelson

8. Economic Evolution
Jack J. Vromen

Rethinking Economic Policy for Social Justice

The radical potential of human rights

Radhika Balakrishnan, James Heintz, and Diane Elson

Routledge
Taylor & Francis Group

LONDON AND NEW YORK

First published 2016
by Routledge
2 Park Square, Milton Park, Abingdon, Oxon OX14 4RN

and by Routledge
711 Third Avenue, New York, NY 10017

Routledge is an imprint of the Taylor & Francis Group, an informa business

British Library Cataloguing in Publication Data
A catalogue record for this book is available from the British
Library

Library of Congress Cataloging in Publication Data
Names: Balakrishnan, Radhika, author. | Heintz, James, author. |
Elson, Diane, author.
Title: Rethinking economic policy for social justice : the radical
potential of human rights / Radhika Balakrishnan, James Heintz
and Diane Elson.
Description: Abingdon, Oxon ; New York, NY : Routledge, 2016.
Identifiers: LCCN 2015040283| ISBN 9781138829145 (hardback) |
ISBN 9781315737911 (ebook) | ISBN 9781138829152 (pbk.)
Subjects: LCSH: Human rights--Economic aspects. | Social
justice--Economic aspects. | Economics--Sociological aspects.
Classification: LCC JC571 .B337 2016 | DDC 330--dc23
LC record available at http://lccn.loc.gov/2015040283

ISBN: 978-1-138-82914-5 (hbk)
ISBN: 978-1-138-82915-2 (pbk)
ISBN: 978-1-315-73791-1 (ebk)

Typeset in Palatino
by Saxon Graphics Ltd, Derby
Printed in Great Britain by Ashford Colour Press Ltd

Contents

Figures

Acknowledgements

Rethinking Economic Policy for Social Justice: The Radical Potential of Human Rights is a culmination of several years of work by the three of us. We would like to thank first and foremost Morgan Campbell who has been an incredible research assistant helping us with background research, giving us substantive comments on chapters and helping pull the manuscript together. We would like to thank Gillian McNoughton, Sam Streed, Stephanie Seguino, and Bhumika Muchhala for their comments on draft chapters.

Radhika Balakrishnan would like to thank Rutgers University for sabbatical time to complete this book; the staff of the Center for Women's Global Leadership for support during this writing process; and David Gillcrist for his continuing support. James Heintz would like to thank the Department of Economics and the Political Economy Research Institute at the University of Massachusetts Amherst for giving him time to work on this volume. Diane Elson would like to thank members of the Human Rights Centre, University of Essex, for helpful discussions over a number of years.

The ideas in this book have been developed over several years of sustained work linking economic analysis to human rights. We have participated in and organized numerous meetings and workshops in collaboration with many organizations, including the Center for Women's Global Leadership (CWGL), the US Human Rights Network, the UN Office of the High Commissioner for Human Rights (OHCHR), the Association for Women's Rights in Development (AWID), and Karama (based in Cairo, Egypt), among others. We would like to thank the participants at these meetings and workshops for their contributions in developing the ideas presented here.

Abbreviations

CEDAW	Convention on the Elimination of All Forms of Discrimination against Women
CERD	Convention on the Elimination of All Forms of Racial Discrimination
CESCR	Committee on Economic, Social and Cultural Rights
CFPB	Consumer Financial Protection Bureau
CRC	Convention on the Rights of the Child
ECB	European Central Bank
ETOs	Extraterritorial Obligations
EU	European Union
FDI	Foreign Direct Investment
FDIC	Federal Deposit Insurance Corporation
FFD	Financing for Development
FTT	Financial Transaction Tax
GATS	General Agreement on Trade in Services
GDP	Gross Domestic Product
GNI	Gross National Income
G20	Group of Twenty
HIPC	Heavily Indebted Poor Country
HRC	Human Rights Council
ICESCR	International Covenant on Economic, Social and Cultural Rights
IFI	International Financial Institutions
IGWG	Intergovernmental Working Group
IMF	International Monetary Fund
LDCs	least developed countries
NGO	Non-Governmental Organization
ODA	Official Development Assistance
OECD	Organization of Economic Cooperation and Development
OHCHR	Office of the High Commissioner for Human Rights
OTC	Over the Counter (derivatives)
PPP	public–private partnership
TARP	Troubled Asset Relief Program

TINTA	There Is No Technocratic Answer
TRIPS	Trade-Related Aspects of Intellectual Property Rights
UDHR	Universal Declaration of Human Rights
UPR	Universal Periodic Review
UN	United Nations
UNDP	United Nations Development Program
UNDRD	United Nations Declaration on the Right to Development
UNDRIP	United Nations Declaration on the Rights of Indigenous Peoples
UNICEF	United Nations Children's Fund
VAT	value added tax
WHO	World Health Organization
WTO	World Trade Organization

1 The radical potential of human rights

Extreme poverty, widespread joblessness, burgeoning inequality, and large-scale environmental threats—addressing these pressing problems requires rethinking economics and economic policy. Yet current approaches to economic policy are not up to this task. Almost everywhere, macroeconomic policy focuses on a handful of narrow goals, such as the growth of gross domestic product or keeping inflation excessively low. A human rights focus provides an alternative normative and evaluative framework that stresses a broader range of objectives that increase the substantive freedoms and choices people enjoy in their lives. These rights include the right to food, the right to work, the right to an adequate standard of living, the right to housing, and the right to education, among others. States have obligations to realize these rights.

Mainstream economics relies on markets to solve the world's problems. It argues that if people and businesses interact in competitive markets, then the most efficient outcome will be achieved. It does not claim that competition will achieve equitable outcomes or a fair distribution of income, but proposes that, by maximizing efficiency, there will be enough gains for winners to compensate losers, should society decide to do so. According to this view, the main purpose of government policy should be to create conditions that allow markets to function efficiently.

But not all economists are the same. Some economists remain skeptical about markets' ability to use resources efficiently. They argue that markets often fail and, in the face of these failures, require corrective action by government. For example, discussions over the causes of the financial and economic crises have centered on the weaknesses of poorly regulated financial markets, and the consequences for society when markets systematically fail (Cassidy 2010). Other economists go beyond money metrics to focus on achievements in capabilities—what people are able to be and do in their lives, such as the capability to be healthy and the capability to read and write.[1] Still others are concerned about the distributive outcomes of economic policies, including the impact on the concentration of income and wealth, gender inequalities, and the vulnerabilities people face.

This book argues that the human rights approach constitutes an alternative evaluative and ethical framework for assessing economic policies and outcomes. The goals of social justice are expressed in terms of the realization of rights—both civil and political rights and also economic, social, and cultural rights. The human rights approach allows for a complex interaction between individual rights, collective rights, and collective action. It sees policy as a social and political process that should conform to human rights standards, not as a purely technocratic exercise. It incorporates an understanding of the paradoxical character of the state, recognizing that states can both enable and deny social justice and that individuals need protection against misuse of state power, as well as requiring the power of the state to be harnessed to realize individual rights. It encompasses a legal framework and provides formal mechanisms through which unjust policy can be contested.

The human rights framework is an evolving one, open-ended rather than closed, and facilitates ongoing discussion and deliberation to address underdeveloped areas and potential deficiencies. The application of human rights treaties to specific contexts and new issues is continually developed by UN human rights treaty bodies, independent experts, academics, and human rights activists. Many human rights principles have potentially important implications for economic governance, yet these possibilities have been underexplored. This book contributes to the process of further developing the human rights framework by exploring the potential it has for transforming the social and economic order within which we live.

Human rights as a framework for social justice

Beginning with the 1948 Universal Declaration of Human Rights (UDHR), followed by the treaties, declarations, and reports stemming from it, human rights have developed through international processes of public reasoning, involving people from all parts of the world. They include not only civil and political rights but also economic, social, and cultural rights. These rights are universal in the sense that they are for everyone—for instance they are for immigrants as well as citizens. These rights are indivisible and interdependent in the sense that civil and political rights cannot be fully secured without guaranteeing the fulfillment of economic, social, and cultural rights, and vice versa. It does not make sense to consider a single right, such as the right to freedom of expression,[2] in isolation. How can freedom of expression be fully realized when some people are denied their right to education?[3] Civil and political rights are essential if governments are to be held to account for their responsibilities to realize economic, social, and cultural rights.

Human rights emphasizes the principle of non-discrimination and equality, addressing specific disadvantages and vulnerabilities based on race, color, sex, language, religion, political or other opinion, national or social origin, property, birth, or other status. The concern with equality extends beyond formal legal equality. A powerful dimension of the human rights framework is that it recognizes the need for substantive equality and that all aspects of people's lives need to be taken into consideration when ensuring that everyone in practice enjoys the same rights and freedoms.

This book focuses primarily on economic and social rights, while recognizing their interdependence with civil and political rights. Economic and social rights are a key part of international law, and they have a strong institutional foundation in the International Covenant on Economic, Social and Cultural Rights (ICESCR), the Convention on the Elimination of All Forms of Discrimination against Women (CEDAW), the Convention on the Elimination of All Forms of Racial Discrimination (CERD), and the UN Declaration on the Right to Development (UNDRD), among others. Some countries—for instance, South Africa—have incorporated these rights into their national constitutions. The majority of the world's countries also have national human rights institutions.[4] Some regions, such as Latin America, have set up regional human rights bodies that include protection of economic and social rights as part of their mandate.

The human rights framework allows us to move beyond a narrow focus on GDP or income when evaluating economic outcomes. Instead, the human rights framework stresses the progressive realization of economic and social rights over time. The idea of progressive realization replaces GDP growth as the measure of social progress. Advances in social justice are achieved when the enjoyment of the rights to an adequate standard of living, education, health, work, and social security improves over time.

Governments can use markets to advance human rights as long as the functioning of markets does not undermine the state's human rights obligations. In mainstream economics, markets are the star players. In the human rights approach, they play a supporting role. To a large extent, this reflects different social objectives and normative frameworks used to evaluate economic policies and institutions. Human rights focuses on progressive improvements in a range of social outcomes, with efficiency being important only insofar as it leads to the greater enjoyment of rights.

Although the human rights framework gives us an alternative to GDP for evaluating outcomes, it does not provide a full prioritization of policy alternatives. Instead, the human rights approach offers guidance in the process of prioritizing alternatives. For example, rights should be progressively realized and steps should be taken to prevent any movement backward in the enjoyment of any particular right. Similarly, the principles of non-discrimination and equality guard against policies that have biased outcomes. However, even when the full array of human rights principles are observed, choices between alternatives must be made. Suppose a government is fully complying with its human rights obligations and suddenly experiences an increase in revenues. Should these resources be spent improving education or health outcomes? Should they be used to reduce debt?

In these cases, the human rights framework does not tell governments which choices are the best. Instead, the state is required to set priorities through a democratically accountable process, while ensuring that its core human rights obligations are met. Securing and protecting civil and political rights are essential for democratic processes to work.

In evaluating economic policy choices, most economists have not engaged with the valuable contribution that the human rights framework can make to the achievement of social justice. An exception is the economist Amartya Sen who has argued that human rights can be seen as ethical criteria for evaluating economic outcomes (Sen 2004; 2009). Sen argues that a human rights approach goes beyond a focus on capabilities alone. It identifies, through a process of public reasoning, which capabilities are to have priority, posing them as rights. It emphasizes that there are obligations to realize these rights, both on the part of individuals and states; and it emphasizes that the procedures adopted to realize the rights must meet certain criteria, such as being equitable (Ibid.).

Therefore, the human rights approach not only provides a normative framework but also procedures for contesting unjust policies that fail to realize rights. These procedures go well beyond juridical processes, although where human rights have been included in constitutions and enacted in national laws, juridical procedures can be used, and an increasing number of cases which pertain to economic and social rights and fiscal policy are being brought to national courts. For instance, in South Africa a case was taken to the Constitutional Court relating to the allocation of resources for housing poor people. The lead plaintiff was Irene Grootboom, who, like many other extremely poor people in Western Cape Province, had nowhere to live. It was claimed that the municipality was failing to provide adequate access to housing. The case was based on two provisions of South Africa's constitution: Section 26, which states that "everyone has right of access to adequate housing" and that the state "must take reasonable legislative and other measures, within its available resources, to achieve progressive realization of this right," and Section 28 (1)(c), which says that children have a right to shelter (Elson 2006).

The case was heard by the South African Constitutional Court, which found that the state's housing program could not be considered reasonable if it did not address the needs of those in extreme conditions of poverty and homelessness. The Court noted that "effective implementation requires at least adequate budgetary support by national government" within the state's available resources. The Court clarified that all three levels of government—national, provincial and local—have obligations to realize the rights to housing. The response of the national government was to develop policy guidelines for the provision of emergency housing and to require the provincial governments to reserve between 0.5 and 0.75

percent of their housing budgets as a contingency fund to meet emergency housing needs (Elson 2006).

In addition, there are many other mechanisms available to hold governments accountable to their human rights obligations. Countries that have ratified a human rights convention are reviewed periodically by international committees of independent experts, who encourage signatories to uphold their international obligations. The Universal Periodic Review (UPR), a peer-review process among members of the United Nations Human Rights Council, examines human rights records across the globe—including countries like the United States who have not ratified many human rights treaties.

The human rights infrastructure can be a powerful advocacy tool with great potential to change policy-making, but only if governments' responsibilities are taken seriously. To realize a vision of an economic system whose purpose is to meet human rights obligations, there is a need to rethink the ways we formulate and evaluate economic policy.

The paradox of the state: duty bearer and arena for struggle

The human rights approach recognizes the complexity of the relation between the state and the people: human rights protect individuals against state action that would violate rights, but state action is also required to fully realize rights. In the human rights framework, the state has the primary responsibility for respecting, promoting, and fulfilling rights. This does not mean that the state is responsible for direct provisioning of all the goods and services that support the realization of rights. The realization of the right to housing does not imply that the state is obligated to supply housing directly, but rather to ensure that public and private institutions work together towards fulfilling the right to housing. The fact that the state is the primary duty bearer does not preclude other institutions—including markets—from playing a central role. However, the state is obligated to take the necessary steps, through policy, legislation, and the judiciary, to support the realization of rights.

These obligations are best discharged by states that are strong, independent of vested interests, well-functioning, and accountable. In practice, of course, there are weak states with limited capacity to secure and protect the enjoyment of rights. Smaller, more dependent economies often lack the policy space to support the realization of rights. Global institutions— like the International Monetary Fund (IMF)—have imposed conditionalities on governments that limit their autonomy and their capacity to meet their obligations.[5] Other states may be strong but have limited democratic accountability. Governments may not make independent decisions, but rather are subject to capture by specific interest groups.

Economic elites and corporate interests can influence government policy and undermine the ability of states to take independent decisions and to be democratically accountable. This can be exacerbated by legal judgments on civil rights (based on national law, not human rights standards). Consider, for instance, the decision of the Supreme Court of the United States with regard to the case of *Citizens United v. the Federal Election Commission*. This ruling eliminated restrictions on corporate donations to electoral campaigns, opening the doors to the unrestricted influence of money in US politics. The ruling effectively gave corporations the same rights as individuals without considering the effect it would have on democratic accountability. This represented yet another US judicial decision in which a justification for protecting a civil right (campaign contributions are considered to be free speech) leads to outcomes that potentially undermine economic and social rights through the influence of powerful individuals and private sector institutions.

There is a fundamental paradox well recognized by the human rights approach. The state is the prime duty bearer for the realization of rights, but it also represents an arena of struggle in which various interests are vying for influence, many of them opposed to realization of human rights. A human rights approach balances faith in the state with skepticism about the state, and ensures that there are procedures to continue to hold the state accountable. In recognizing the paradoxes of the state, the human rights approach provides an important corrective to the ideas about the state implicit in much economic policy analysis.

Individual rights, collective rights, and collective action

Many mainstream human rights organizations have highly selective readings of human rights that only focus on civil and political rights without adequately considering economic and social rights. On the other hand, human rights are often criticized by some outside the mainstream as being overly individualistic and, therefore, feeding into neoliberal ideologies that cast the challenge of social justice narrowly, in terms of protecting and advancing individual choices.

Human rights are indeed about individual freedoms. This is a critical aspect of the way human rights frames issues of social justice. But the human rights framework insists that full realization of these rights requires a strong state, international cooperation and robust social institutions. It recognizes that claiming individual rights demands collective action and responsibility. The human rights approach ensures individual freedoms—including economic, social, and cultural rights, as well as civil and political rights. But there must be a collective responsibility, exercised through the state, and through cooperation between states for realizing these individual rights.

The interdependence of individual and collective rights is addressed in a variety of human rights instruments. For example, the Universal Declaration of Human Rights specifically states that everyone has the right to form and join trade unions (Article 23) so that actions that prevent workers from collectively organizing are infringements of their human rights. The Declaration on the Right to Development (1986) includes the right of peoples to self-determination and sovereignty over land and resources.[6] It states, "The right to development is an inalienable human right by virtue of which every human person and all peoples are entitled to participate in, contribute to, and enjoy economic, social, cultural and political development, in which all human rights and fundamental freedoms can be fully realized." The United Nations Declaration on the Rights of Indigenous Peoples (UNDRIP) recognizes from the start that for indigenous peoples, human rights must go beyond the individual to recognize the communities to which they belong. The rights of the collective in terms of indigenous peoples are defined with regard to preserving rights to land, language, and culture. However, it is important to recognize that even in the presence of these collective rights, the rights of the individual are protected.

Looking at a collective often misses the needs of social groups such as women, racial and ethnic groups, and the disabled. The human rights approach ensures that, even in the presence of these collective rights, the rights of the individual are protected, and treaties like CERD and CEDAW are operative to protect the rights of those who for reasons of race and gender may be discriminated against by the collective.

Human rights-based approaches to social justice have been subject to other critiques. For example, some have argued that the current construction of human rights is culturally biased, is therefore not universal in nature, and should not be used to assess social justice.[7] However, evidence suggests that arguments about fundamental differences over the basic values inherent in human rights are often exaggerated.[8] In addition, the Universal Declaration of Human Rights was drafted by representatives with different cultural backgrounds from all regions of the world and was adopted in 1948 with no objections by any member countries.[9] Other critiques stress that the discourse of human rights may be co-opted and used to reinforce the exercise of imperialist power at a global level, such as military interventions justified on the basis of the need to protect rights (Kennedy 2005).

While these concerns over the use of human rights discourse must be taken into account, they primarily focus on how human rights have been appropriated and misused. There is a need to resist this misappropriation because the human rights framework can provide a powerful tool for making far-reaching advances in social justice. The argument we make in this book is that human rights are potentially transformative and have enormous implications for how we organize and govern our economies.

TINTA: human rights and setting priorities

The dominant approach in economics tends to focus on technical evaluations of outcomes to determine which ones are the "best." This approach typically uses tools, such as cost-benefit analyses, which quantify the costs and benefits of particular interventions in order to rank or evaluate outcomes, and economic models that assess the impact of different policies.[10] The human rights framework does not give us a neat ranking of policy options based on technical analysis, but instead stresses that policy processes must be accountable, participatory, and transparent. It relies on well-informed democratic processes, grounded in human rights law, to evaluate policy options. In the human rights framework, "there is no technocratic answer"—which we can sum up with the acronym TINTA. Democratic participation is essential and meaningful participation requires the protection of the basic rights of all people, such as the freedom of expression, the right to liberty, and the right to take part in the government of their country.

Amartya Sen reflected on the role of the state and democratic participation in the context of the 2008 financial crisis and the subsequent austerity policies adopted by many countries, drawing on Adam Smith's early writing:

> The father of modern economics, and the pioneering champion of the market system, did not have any doubt why the role of the state fits integrally into the demands of a good society. Public reasoning over generations has increasingly vindicated and supported Adam Smith's broad vision. There are good reasons to think that it would have done the same today had open and informed public dialogue been given a proper chance, rather than being ruled out by the alleged superiority of the judgments of financial leaders, with their breathtakingly narrow view of human society and a basic lack of interest in the demands of a deliberative democracy.
>
> (Sen 2015)

It is, however, very important that public dialogue and democratic deliberations be informed by knowledge of alternative economic policies, human rights, and the obligations of government to realize these rights. Otherwise, deliberations may result in the adoption of policies that are no better, in terms of fulfilling rights, than those representing the interests of small, but powerful constituencies, such as the financial sector.[11]

The transformative potential of human rights

Because of the role of collective interests and those who control economic resources in determining policy priorities and social outcomes, the full realization of rights represents a fundamental challenge to the way our economy is currently organized and governed. Michal Kalecki, an economist at Cambridge University from the 1930s to the 1960s, wrote an essay called "The Political Aspects of Full Employment" in which he argued that a capitalist system would never move towards full employment, since it would undermine the economic power and social position of businesses and the owners of capital relative to working people (Kalecki 1943). In other words, the full realization of the right to work would require a different type of economy. We can extend this argument to the full array of human rights—health, education, employment, social security, and housing, to name a few. The full realization of these rights would challenge existing social stratifications, inequalities, and power relationships. There is bound to be pushback from those in more privileged positions and the realization of rights is fundamentally a political struggle for a different social order.

Article 28 of the Universal Declaration of Human Rights states that "everyone is entitled to a social and international order in which the rights and freedoms set forth in this Declaration can be fully realized." The current social and international order fails in guaranteeing these fundamental freedoms. To move from the current situation to an order that supports the full realization of rights, the ways in which economies function and the approach to economic policy must be transformed. This book explores the radical potential of the human rights framework and the implications it has for transforming the social and economic order within which we live.

Structure of the book

Chapter 2 presents a summary of the elements of a human rights approach—specifically the various principles and obligations reflected in international declarations, conventions, and treaties—and their implications for economic policy. One of the major concerns facing the world today is the unprecedented increase in social and economic inequality. Chapter 3 explores the implications of the human rights framework for evaluating and addressing issues of economic and social inequality across multiple dimensions.

Chapters 4 and 5 discuss a central obligation imposed by international economic and social rights law: namely, the requirement under Article 2(1) of the International Covenant on Economic, Social and Cultural Rights (ICESCR) that governments deploy the maximum of their available resources toward the realization of economic and social rights. Chapter 4 focuses on government expenditure and tax policy in light of the human rights principle of using the maximum of available resources. Chapter 5 expands on these issues, looking in depth at monetary policy, debt, and development assistance.

The process of financialization refers to the growing influence of financial institutions and interests in our economies and societies. Chapter 6 analyzes the role financial institutions and credit markets play in the realization of, or failure to realize, human rights. Our economies are increasingly interconnected. These days the actions by governments and corporations in one country affect the realization of rights elsewhere. The human rights framework is beginning to address these realities by acknowledging that states may have "extraterritorial obligations." In Chapter 7, we examine these relationships and their implications for economic policy, global governance, and the realization of economic and social rights. Finally, Chapter 8 explores the relationship between economic and financial instability and human rights—including policy responses to economic crises.

Notes

1 Sen (2012) makes it clear that not all capabilities are important and of ethical value, and that the identification of those that are to be included in normative frameworks should be decided through processes of public reasoning.
2 Included in Universal Declaration of Human Rights, Article 19.
3 Included in Universal Declaration of Human Rights, Article 26.
4 An example of a national human rights institution is the South African Human Rights Commission, which educates people about human rights, investigates potential violations, and proposes remedies.
5 Although the IMF is not a party to the fundamental international agreements on human rights, member states should guarantee that IMF policies are conducive to the realization of human rights.
6 The use of the plural "peoples" is significant and is there in recognition that people are not just individuals.
7 See, for example, Mutua (2001) who argues that traditional human rights discourse creates "savages," "victims," and "saviors," which reinforces existing global stratifications (e.g. the saviors are represented by governments and human rights organizations in the global north that attempt to rescue victims from savages in the global south).
8 Sen (2004) discusses these claims and provides historical examples that counteract the idea that the values of different parts of the world can be confined in these boxes. He concludes that "not only are the differences on the subject of freedoms and rights that actually exist between different societies often much exaggerated, but also there is, typically, little note taken of substantial variations *within* each local culture" (Sen 2004, p. 353).
9 Eight countries abstained from the vote in the UN General Assembly when the Universal Declaration was adopted. All other member countries voted for adoption.
10 In fact, value judgements are often smuggled into these technocratic exercises. For instance, evaluations of spending on programs that are designed to cut human fatalities, such as traffic management programs or health interventions, put a value on lives saved in terms of the estimated lifetime earnings of those kept alive. Thus, the lives of younger high-earners are valued much more than those of older low-earning people, retired people, and people who cannot work because of disabilities.

11 These dynamics were evident in the case of deliberations in the German parliament in 2015 over the terms of additional EU lending to Greece. See, for instance, reports on *BBC News*, including www.bbc.co.uk/news/world-europe-33984008 [Accessed 18 Aug. 2015].

References

Cassidy, J. (2010). *How Markets Fail: The Logic of Economic Calamities*. New York: Picador.

Elson, D. (2006). *Budgeting for Women's Rights: Monitoring Government Budgets for Compliance with CEDAW*. New York: UNIFEM. Available at: http://es.unrol.org/doc.aspx?n=MonitoringGovernmentBudgetsComplianceCEDAW_eng.pdf [Accessed 12 Sept. 2015].

Kalecki, M. (1943). The political aspects of full employment. *Political Quarterly* 4, pp. 322–31.

Kennedy, D. (2005). *The Dark Side of Virtue: Reassessing International Humanitarianism*. Princeton, NJ: Princeton University Press.

Mutua, W. M. (2001). Savages, victims, and saviors: The metaphor of human rights. *Harvard International Law Journal* 42(1), pp. 201–45.

Sen, A. (2004). Elements of a theory of human rights. *Philosophy and Public Affairs* 32(4), pp. 315–56.

Sen, A. (2009). *The Idea of Justice*. London: Penguin and Cambridge, MA: Harvard University Press.

Sen, A. (2012). 'Foreword' in D. Elson, P. Vizard and S. Fukuda-Parr, eds., *Human Rights and the Capabilities Approach*. London and New York: Routledge, pp. viii–x.

Sen, A. (2015). The economic consequences of austerity. *New Statesman* [online]. Available at: http://www.newstatesman.com/politics/2015/06/amartya-sen-economic-consequences-austerity [Accessed 11 Sept. 2015].

United Nations Declaration on the Right to Development. (1986). Resolution 41/128. Available at: http://www.un.org/documents/ga/res/41/a41r128.htm [Accessed 26 Sept. 2015].

United Nations Declaration on the Rights of Indigenous Peoples. (2007). Available at: http://www.un.org/esa/socdev/unpfii/documents/DRIPS_en.pdf [Accessed 26 Sept. 2015].

Universal Declaration of Human Rights. (1948). Available at: http://www.ohchr.org/EN/UDHR/Documents/UDHR_Translations/eng.pdf.

2 The human rights framework and economic policy

Human rights are a set of internationally agreed-upon norms and standards, covering economic, social, and cultural rights, as well as civil and political rights, that take as their point of departure the opening words of the 1948 Universal Declaration of Human Rights (UDHR): "All human beings are born free and equal in dignity and rights." The preamble to the Declaration states that its purpose is to proclaim human rights

> as a common standard of achievement for all peoples, and all nations, to the end that every individual and every organ of society, keeping this Declaration constantly in mind, shall strive by teaching and education to promote respect for these rights and freedoms and by progressive measures, national and international, to secure their universal and effective recognition and observance.

This makes it clear that while the ethical starting point is recognition that everyone has human rights, the realization of these rights is a complex and difficult process that goes well beyond the enactment of laws. Human rights provides standards by which we can judge not only existing laws but also institutions and policies; set out goals for economic, social, and political change; and build broad social movements that can hold governments to account for fulfilling their obligations to realize human rights.

This chapter sets out the key dimensions of human rights obligations and the key human rights principles that are especially relevant to economic policy analysis. It explains the system of human rights treaties; the operation of the United Nations (UN) committees that monitor compliance with treaties; and the work of the Special Rapporteurs who investigate specific problems in realization of human rights. Drawing upon the treaties, and the General Comments/Recommendations of the treaty bodies, and the reports of expert groups of human rights lawyers, this chapter establishes a framework for formulating and assessing economic policy, with particular reference to the International Covenant on Economic, Social and Cultural Rights (ICESCR), the Convention on the Elimination of All Forms of Racial Discrimination (CERD) and the

Convention on the Elimination of All Forms of Discrimination against Women (CEDAW).[1]

The human rights system[2]

The Universal Declaration of Human Rights has been embodied in a series of international treaties, variously known as Conventions or Covenants, which set out rights in more detail, and the obligations of states to realize those rights. Here we focus mainly on the International Covenant on Economic, Social and Cultural Rights (ICESCR 1966), the Convention on the Elimination of All Forms of Racial Discrimination (CERD 1969) and the Convention on the Elimination of All Forms of Discrimination against Women (CEDAW 1979). A sizeable majority of the world's countries are parties to these treaties and, for these countries, the treaties are legally binding.

The UN operates a system for monitoring compliance with these treaties: states have to make periodic reports in relation to each treaty to an international committee of independent experts that issues a comment drawing attention to areas of non-compliance. For instance, the Committee on Economic, Social and Cultural Rights (CESCR) is the UN body that monitors the implementation of ICESCR and considers the periodic reports that states that have ratified ICESCR are required to submit. The CEDAW Committee is the UN body that monitors the implementation of CEDAW and considers the periodic reports that states that have ratified CEDAW are required to submit. These treaty bodies, as the committees are known, also issue General Comments, or, in some cases, Recommendations, clarifying various aspects of the treaties and indicating how they are to be interpreted in light of current events.

The overarching body is the Human Rights Council, established in 2006,[3] an inter-governmental body within the UN system responsible for strengthening the promotion and protection of human rights around the globe and for addressing situations of human rights violations and making recommendations on them. It has the ability to discuss all thematic human rights issues and situations that require its attention throughout the year. The Council has an advisory committee which functions as its think tank and a complaints procedure where individuals and organizations can bring cases of violation of human rights to the Council. One of its responsibilities is the Universal Periodic Review, through which it reviews the compliance with human rights obligations of all member states, regardless of what convention or treaty that government has ratified. The Special Procedures branch also falls under the umbrella of the Council and includes Special Rapporteurs, special representatives, independent experts, and working groups that monitor, examine, advise, and publicly report on thematic issues or human rights situations in specific countries.

National and international non-governmental organizations are quick to use the reports and Concluding Observations and General Comments/ Recommendations issued by UN human rights bodies in their campaigns, and can themselves submit "shadow reports" to treaty bodies. Increasingly, NGOs concerned with economic and social rights are analyzing economic policies from a human rights point of view, including in Guatemala, Spain, and Ireland (Saiz 2013).

Human rights obligations

The treaties that stem from UDHR set out the obligations of governments towards human rights. These obligations have been spelled out more fully through a number of mechanisms, including General Comments and Recommendations issued from time to time by UN treaty monitoring bodies and by experts in international law, such as the groups of experts who produced the Limburg Principles on the Implementation of the International Covenant on Economic, Social and Cultural Rights (1986), the Maastricht Guidelines on Violations of Economic, Social and Cultural Rights (1997), and the Maastricht Principles on Extraterritorial Obligations of States in the Area of Economic, Social and Cultural Rights (2012).

The obligations of states that are party to ICESCR are set out in more detail in General Comment 3, "The nature of States parties' obligations" (CESCR 1990). They include obligations of conduct and of result. These obligations are further clarified in the Maastricht Guidelines on Violations of Economic, Social and Cultural Rights,[4] which identify three dimensions of these obligations (OHCHR 2005, Annex 5):

- the obligation to respect requires States to refrain from interfering with the enjoyment of economic, social and cultural rights. Thus the right to housing is violated if the State engages in arbitrary forced evictions;
- the obligation to protect requires States to prevent violations of such rights by third parties. Thus the failure to ensure that private employers comply with basic labor standards may amount to a violation of the right to work or the right to just and favorable conditions of work;
- the obligation to fulfil requires States to take appropriate legislative, administrative, budgetary, judicial and other measures towards the full realization of such rights. Thus, the failure of States to provide essential primary health care to those in need may amount to a violation.

Furthermore the Maastricht Guidelines state that:

The obligations to respect, protect and fulfil each contain elements of obligation of conduct and obligation of result. The obligation of conduct requires action reasonably calculated to realize the enjoyment of a particular right. In the case of the right to health, for example, the obligation of conduct could involve the adoption and implementation of a plan of action to reduce maternal mortality. The obligation of result requires States to achieve specific targets to satisfy a detailed substantive standard [of realization of the relevant right].

(OHCHR 2005, p. 118)

As recognized in para 8 of the Guidelines, governments enjoy some discretion in selecting the means for implementing their respective obligations. These obligations clearly have implications for economic analysis and policy-making. They open a space in which the extent to which policy is based on "reasonable calculations" can be assessed and outcomes related to a range of rights can be evaluated, instead of relying on a single narrow indicator, such as economic growth. Human rights experts have not specified in any detail what makes a calculation "reasonable," but some general principles have been identified and these are discussed in the next section. However, the mere act of framing economic policy in terms of human rights helps to change the terms of public debate on economic policy. For instance, the elimination of poverty becomes more than a charitable goal. It becomes a duty of the state (Hertel and Minkler 2007).

Although states have accepted these obligations, they rarely bear human rights in mind in the design or implementation of their economic policies. Human rights are typically seen as the responsibility of ministries like the Justice Ministry, not of the Finance Ministry. However, at the UN World Conference on Human Rights in Vienna in 1993, governments did recognize that human rights are "the first responsibility of governments" (United Nations 1993, para 1).

The obligations of states extend beyond their own borders, as is made clear in the UN Charter, Articles 55 and 56. Obligations with respect to international development co-operation between governments are explicitly referred to in Article 2 of ICESCR, and underlined in specific provisions in Article 11 (the right to an adequate standard of living). Articles 22 and 23 specifically refer to the need for international measures. In 1990, CESCR General Comment 3 explicitly stated that: "international co-operation for development … is an obligation of all States." The UN High Commissioner for Human Rights has subsequently produced a number of reports on trade and investment clarifying that international trade and investment agreements must be consistent with the human rights obligations of states.[5] The Declaration on the Right to Development, UNDRD (1986), also recognizes the need for international cooperation. The Maastricht Principles on Extraterritorial Obligations of States in the Area of Economic, Social and Cultural Rights (Maastricht University and International Commission of Jurists 2011) recognize that policies adopted by governments have an impact on the realization of economic and social rights beyond their own borders. They clarify that governments have human rights obligations regarding this impact, for instance, obligations regarding the regulation of multinational corporations and global finance as discussed in detail in Chapter 7.

Intergovernmental organizations are also bound by human rights norms and standards. UN organizations such as UNICEF, UN-Women, and the World Health Organization (WHO) have organized much of their work in relation to the Convention on the Rights of the Child (CRC), the Convention on the Elimination of All Forms of Discrimination against Women (CEDAW), and the Right to Health, respectively. In 2013 the UN Secretary General adopted a "Human Rights Up Front" policy calling upon all UN agencies, funds, and programs to treat human rights as a system-wide core responsibility (Alston 2015a, p. 16). The World Bank has not yet accepted such a responsibility. The current Special Rapporteur on Extreme Poverty and Human Rights, Philip Alston, found that the World Bank pays lip service to human rights but does not generally engage with human rights in its operations and lending (Ibid., p. 15). He recommends that the World Bank should adopt a human rights policy that will guide its operations, avoiding an approach that seeks to impose sanctions on borrowing states in response to human rights violations, and instead seeks to encourage and assist governments in meeting their human rights obligations. It must ensure that the Bank's own policies and projects do no harm and are in compliance with human rights standards.

Human rights principles relevant for economic analysis and policy

States enjoy a margin of discretion in selecting the means to carry out their human rights obligations. In discharging their obligations for realization of economic and social rights, states must pay regard to Article 2.1 of the 1966 International Covenant on Economic, Social and Cultural Rights (ICESCR) which states that:

> Each State Party to the present Covenant undertakes to take steps, individually and through international assistance and co-operation, especially economic and technical, to the maximum of its available resources, with a view to achieving progressively the full realization of the rights recognized in the present Covenant by all appropriate means, including particularly the adoption of legislative measures.

In addition to the principle of progressive realization using maximum available resources, states must take into account the following additional key points, specified in General Comment 3 (CESCR 1990): the avoidance of retrogression; the satisfaction of minimum essential levels of economic and social rights; and non-discrimination and equality. In addition, the principles of participation, transparency and accountability must be adhered to as specified in the Limburg Principles on the Implementation of the ICESCR (OHCHR 2005, Annex 6). These principles can be used as a framework for analyzing and designing economic policy.

Progressive realization

The ICESCR (1966), Article 2, specifies that states parties have the obligation of "achieving progressively the full realization of the rights recognized in the present Covenant to the maximum of available resources." This obligation does recognize that the resources at the disposition of a government are not unlimited, and that fulfilling economic and social rights will take time. At the same time, the concept of "progressive realization" is not intended to take away all "meaningful content" of a state's obligation to realize economic, social, and cultural rights:

> The Committee on Economic, Social and Cultural Rights, in General Comment 3, has clarified "progressive realization" as follows:
>   The concept of progressive realization constitutes a recognition of the fact that full realization of all economic, social and cultural rights will generally not be able to be achieved in a short period of time. In this sense the obligation differs significantly from that contained in Article 2 of the International Covenant on Civil and Political Rights which embodies an immediate obligation to respect and ensure all of the relevant rights. Nevertheless, the fact that realization over time, or in other words progressively, is foreseen under the Covenant should not be misinterpreted as depriving the obligation of all meaningful content. It is on the one hand a necessary flexibility device, reflecting the realities of the real world and the difficulties involved for any country in ensuring full realization of economic, social and cultural rights. On the other hand, the phrase must be read in the light of the overall objective, indeed the raison d'être, of the Covenant which is to establish clear obligations for States parties in respect of the full realization of the rights in question. It thus imposes an obligation to move as expeditiously and effectively as possible towards that goal.
> (CESRC 1990, General Comment 3, para 9)

These steps toward full realization of rights must be "taken within a reasonably short time after the Covenant's entry into force for the States concerned" and such steps should be "deliberate, concrete and targeted as clearly as possible" in order to meet the obligations of states (Ibid., para 2).

Non-retrogression

The CESCR (1990) has stated in General Comment 3, paragraph 9, that there is a strong presumption that actions by the government that lead to a deterioration in the enjoyment of economic and social rights are not permitted:

> Moreover, any deliberately retrogressive measures in that regard would require the most careful consideration and would need to be fully justified by reference to the totality of the rights provided for in the Covenant and in the context of the full use of the maximum available resources.

An example of a potentially retrogressive measure would be cuts to expenditures on public services, like health and education, that are critical for realization of economic and social rights, especially if spending in other areas, such as military spending, is not cut equivalently.

Minimum essential levels/minimum core obligations

States that are parties to the ICESCR are also under a "minimum core" obligation to ensure the satisfaction of, at the very least, "minimum essential levels of each of the rights" in the ICESCR. This means that a state party in which any "significant number" of persons is "deprived of essential foodstuffs, of essential primary health care, etc. is prima facie failing to meet obligations" under the Covenant (CESCR 1990, General Comment 3, para 10). The Committee on Economic, Social and Cultural Rights has clarified that this is a continuing obligation, requiring states with inadequate resources to strive to ensure enjoyment of rights (Ibid., para 11). However, even in times of severe resource constraints, states must ensure that rights are fulfilled for vulnerable members of society (Ibid., para 12). The Committee on Economic, Social and Cultural Rights has begun to identify the content of the minimum core obligations with respect to the rights to food, education, health, and water (CESCR (1999a); (1999c); (2000); and (2003), respectively) though it has not specified this in quantitative terms.

Ensuring the satisfaction of minimum essential levels is an immediate obligation. This means that it is the duty of the state to prioritize the rights of the poorest and most vulnerable people. Nevertheless, this does not imply that states must adopt a very narrowly targeted approach, using special programs that are only for the very poor. The Committee on Economic, Social and Cultural Rights has emphasized that "the obligation remains for a State party to strive to ensure the widest possible enjoyment of the relevant rights" (CESCR 1990, General Comment 3, para 11). Several

UN Special Rapporteurs have highlighted the importance of broad-based systems as the best way to meet minimum core obligations.

Non-discrimination and equality

A fundamental aspect of states' human rights obligations is that of non-discrimination and equality. The Universal Declaration of Human Rights, Article 2, states that:

> Everyone is entitled to all the rights and freedoms set forth in this Declaration without distinction of any kind, such as race, colour, sex, language, religion, political or other opinion, national or social origin, property, birth or other status.

The same language is used in ICESCR (1966) in Article 2. Several human rights treaties specifically deal with non-discrimination in relation to particular categories of people. For instance, CEDAW prohibits discrimination against women in all its forms and obligates states to condemn this discrimination and take steps "by all appropriate means and without delay" to pursue a policy of eliminating this discrimination (Article 2). Article 2 of CEDAW (1979) also sets out steps that a state party must take to eliminate this discrimination, including adopting appropriate legislative and other measures. Article 4, para 1 recognizes the legitimacy of "temporary special measures aimed at accelerating de facto equality between men and women." It is clear that CEDAW does not only mean the absence of a discriminatory legal framework, but also means that policies must not be discriminatory in effect. CEDAW requires that states achieve both substantive and formal equality and recognizes that formal equality alone is insufficient for a state to meet its affirmative obligation to achieve substantive equality between men and women (CEDAW 2004, General Recommendation 25, para 8).

In the same vein, the International Convention on the Elimination of All Forms of Racial Discrimination (CERD 1969), Article 2, requires that states parties condemn racial discrimination and pursue by all appropriate means and without delay a policy of eliminating racial discrimination in all its forms. The state is also obliged to take special and concrete measures to ensure the adequate development and protection of certain racial groups or individuals belonging to them, for the purpose of guaranteeing them the full and equal enjoyment of human rights and fundamental freedoms. These measures cannot maintain unequal or separate rights for different racial groups (CERD 1969, Article 2, para 2). CERD (1969, Article 5, para e) further elaborates that in compliance with the fundamental obligations laid down in Article 2, of this Convention, governments must undertake to prohibit and eliminate racial discrimination in all its forms and to guarantee the right of everyone—without distinction as to race, color, or national or ethnic origin—to equality before the law, notably in the enjoyment of economic, social, and cultural rights.

Less attention has been paid to the fact that both UDHR and ICESCR specify "property" among the grounds on which distinction in the enjoyment of rights is not permitted. MacNaughton (2009) points out that it has been accepted that this refers to the wealth or poverty status of people, and that distinction on the basis of wealth or poverty very often overlaps with distinction on the basis of other statuses, such as race and ethnic origin. Poor people are often disproportionately from particular status groups.

The Committee on Economic, Social and Cultural Rights has made it clear that the recognition that realization will be "progressive" does not provide states with an excuse for the persistence of discrimination. States have an obligation to "guarantee" that there will be no discrimination in the exercise of rights (see: ICESCR 1966, Article 2, para 2; CESCR 1990, General Comment 3, para 2; CESCR 1999b, General Comment 12, para 43; CESCR 2000, General Comment 14, para 31; CESCR 2003, General Comment 15, para 17). This means that non-discrimination must always be a priority in the progressive realization of economic, social, and cultural rights and that any steps that a state takes to progressively realize such rights must be non-discriminatory in both policy and effect. Like ensuring satisfaction of minimum essential levels of economic and social rights, non-discrimination is an immediate obligation.

Accountability, transparency, and participation

Governments should be accountable, both to the international community and to their own people, for their compliance with the obligations under human rights treaties. The Committee on Economic, Social and Cultural Rights has emphasized that "rights and obligation demand accountability . . . whatever the mechanisms of accountability, they must be accessible, transparent and effective" (CESCR 2001, para 14). Central to transparency is the right to information, specified in Article 19 of the Universal Declaration of Human Rights and further elaborated in Article 19 of the International Covenant on Civil and Political Rights.

The Committee on Economic, Social and Cultural Rights has also indicated that the right of individuals to participate must be an "integral component" of any policy or practice that seeks to meet the state obligation to ensure the equal right of men and women to the enjoyment of all human rights (2005, General Comment 16, para 37).[6] CEDAW requires that women be able to participate on equal terms with men in decision-making about the budget. Article 7(a) calls for women to participate equally in the formulation of government policy and its implementation and to hold public office and perform all public functions; and Article 7(b) calls for women to participate in non-governmental organizations and associations which address the state's public and political life.

Maximum available resources

The definition of the "maximum available resources," which the government should utilize for "progressive realization" of human rights, has not yet been fully elaborated by the Committee on Economic, Social and Cultural Rights. The Committee issued a statement in 2007 entitled "An Evaluation of the Obligation to Take Steps to the 'Maximum of Available Resources' Under an Optional Protocol to the Covenant." However, the statement did not define what constitutes available resources, beyond stating that it refers to "both the resources existing within a state as well as those available from the international community through international cooperation and assistance" (CESCR 2007). The concept of maximum available resources requires further development in order to demonstrate that governments must mobilize resources, not simply administer existing resources, in order to meet human rights obligations. The principle of maximum available resources applies to all resources available to the government—including natural, human, and technical resources. Here we focus on financial resources.

Several treaty bodies, Special Rapporteurs, and independent experts have pointed to the importance of taxation in mobilizing the maximum available resources (Balakrishnan and Elson 2008). For instance, the Special Rapporteur on the Right to Education has noted that taxes are essential for any state to raise the revenue needed to finance health, education, infrastructure, or assistance for those too young or too old to work (Tomasevski 1998). Philip Alston, Special Rapporteur on Extreme Poverty, commented on the links between taxation and the realization of rights:

> Refusing to levy taxes, or failing to collect them, both of which are commonplace in many countries, results in the availability of inadequate revenue to fund human rights related expenditures … tax policy is where the action really is in terms of setting priorities. Tax policies reflect better than all of the ministerial statements and white papers the real priorities of a government. We can see clearly the activities that it chooses to incentivize, those that it opts to disincentivize, the groups that it decides to privilege, and the groups that it decides to ignore or even penalize.
>
> (Alston, 2015b, p. 1)

Of course, the system of taxation must be organized so as to comply with human rights standards. Tomasevski (2005) notes that the European Court of Human Rights has legitimized the power of states to levy taxes, provided that judicial remedies exist to prevent taxation amounting to arbitrary confiscation. Taxation must also be non-discriminatory between different social groups, such as women and men.

There are other policy areas, in addition to government spending and taxation, which affect the resources available to government to support the realization of rights. These include development assistance, debt and deficit financing, and monetary policies.[7] Concerns over the impact of high levels of indebtedness on the fulfillment of rights led to the appointment of an Independent Expert on the Effects of Debt on Human Rights. The reports of the independent expert examine the implications of accumulated debt on the governments' ability to meet their human rights obligations. However, it is also important to recognize that borrowing can also have a positive impact on human rights. Well-chosen borrowing to finance public investments in education, health, nutrition, and infrastructure helps to realize human rights and can also generate the revenues to service the loans by raising productivity and economic growth. Furthermore, borrowing can prevent retrogression when government revenues unexpectedly decline—for instance, in the face of a significant economic shock.

Many of these aspects of maximum available resources correspond to what some economists refer to as the "fiscal space diamond" (UNDP 2010). The four points of the diamond are expenditure reprioritization and efficiency; domestic resource mobilization through taxation and other revenue raising measures; foreign aid grants (Official Development Assistance, ODA); and deficit financing. In addition, monetary and financial policies provide potentially powerful instruments for directing financial resources toward uses that support the realization of human rights. Monetary policy, conducted by central banks, influences the resources available to realize rights, for instance through its impact on the level of employment. However, the extent to which the mandate and practices of the central bank are consistent with human rights obligations is rarely considered. There is no reason why central banks should not be held accountable to the same human rights principles as other government agencies (Heintz 2012).

Therefore, maximum available resources should be examined in terms of five types of policy: (1) government expenditure; (2) government revenue; (3) development assistance (both official development assistance and private resource flows); (4) debt and deficit financing; and (5) monetary policy and financial regulation (Balakrishnan et al. 2011). Together, these interrelated policy areas can be represented in a diagram with five critical nodes for mobilizing resources, shown in Figure 2.1. These issues are discussed in much greater depth in Chapters 4 and 5.

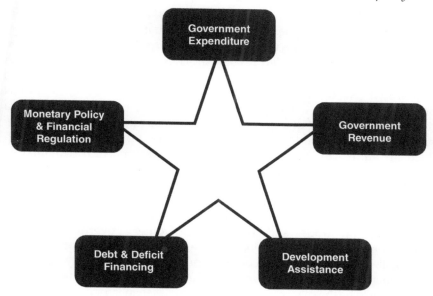

Figure 2.1 Maximum available resources

Auditing economic policy in light of human rights obligations

The human rights framework can be used to audit economic policies and distinguish between obligations of conduct (what policies were adopted) and obligations of result—how far are economic and social rights being realized (Balakrishnan and Elson 2008). There are a number of steps to conduct a policy audit: first, select the economic policies to be considered; second, identify the human rights principles that apply to the selected policies; third, identify relevant indicators to assess how far obligations of conduct are being met; and finally identify indicators of results in realizing economic and social rights, and crosscheck with indicators of conduct.

In choosing indicators, it is important to take into account the country context. It would not be appropriate to compare countries with different levels of wealth against the same set of results using some absolute standard (e.g. full enrolment of all children in school). So indicators should focus on benchmarking with comparable countries; benchmarking in the same country over time; and benchmarking between social groups in the same country.

It is important to draw a distinction between an audit and a study of policy impact. The latter purports to establish a causal link between economic policies and the degree of substantive enjoyment of economic and social rights ("results"). Impact studies require the use of mathematical models and econometric techniques, combined with assumptions about "counter-factuals" (i.e. about what would have happened if different economic policies had been used). The technical apparatus of studies that purport to examine impact often obscure the nature of the guesstimates that have been made in constructing the counter-factuals. Moreover, no impact study can definitely establish causation, but only establish correlation and suggest plausible reasons for interpreting this as evidence of causation. An audit has a less ambitious aim: to examine how policy has been conducted—has it consisted of action "reasonably calculated to realize the enjoyment of a particular right," selecting rights which might reasonably be thought to have a strong relation to the policy instrument. Such an audit can use both quantitative indicators and a qualitative examination of relevant legislation and policy processes, relating them to the obligation of conduct and the obligation of result.

It is important to examine not only the conduct of the state in question, but also the extent to which it is enabled or constrained by international agreements on trade and finance with other governments, with international financial institutions, and with multinational corporations. Responsibility for any shortcomings may not rest entirely with the government in question, but may be shared with other bodies. This is more likely to be the case in poor, small countries than in rich and powerful ones, but even in the latter, multinational corporations may share some of the responsibility.

An example of auditing economic policy: the case of trade policy

Many economists argue that trade liberalization will produce gains in the form of extra output by stimulating economies to be more efficient. Not all economists agree. Some doubt that trade liberalization will necessarily lead to overall gains. The gains from trade may be unequally distributed, with some countries actually being made worse off. In addition, not all groups within a country will necessarily gain from trade. Some trade agreements include provisions in areas such as labor rights, intellectual property rights, and government subsidies. When evaluating trade policies, it is important to consider whose rights have been weakened and whose rights have been strengthened.

Consider an audit of a trade agreement based on the human rights principle of non-discrimination and equality. In auditing the obligation of conduct, it is important to investigate whether the government conducted impact assessments to determine who will be the likely winners and losers before concluding trade agreements. If the likely losers were groups already subject to discrimination and inequality, did the government ensure that the trade agreement was modified to protect them? Or failing modification of the trade agreement, did the government introduce other measures to compensate them for their losses? Moreover, some trade agreements require legislative changes at the national level to comply with the terms of the agreement. The implications of these policy changes need to be taken into account.

In auditing the obligation of result, indicators are required on the situation of different social groups before and after the adoption of the trade agreement. If a trade agreement worsens the position of those who are already suffering from discrimination and inequality, then measures should be taken to prevent this. Compliance with obligations is questionable if the state failed to make an impact assessment and failed to introduce safeguards or compensatory measures to protect discriminated against groups from losses, and if the situation of vulnerable groups worsens after trade liberalization. Responsibility may be shared with powerful trading partners if the latter refused to include safeguards in the trade agreements and limited access to their own markets in ways that minimized any gains from trade.

Conclusions

This chapter has established that states have obligations with respect to economic and social rights. The obligation of conduct requires action reasonably calculated to realize the enjoyment of a particular right. The obligation of result requires governments to achieve specific standards of realization of the right. This chapter has also identified key human rights principles that can be used to formulate and assess the conduct and results of economic policy: progressive realization; use of maximum available resources; avoidance of retrogression; the satisfaction of minimum essential levels of economic and social rights; the achievement of non-discrimination and equality; and participation, transparency, and accountability.

The human rights perspective is rooted in the view that human beings require minimum levels of income and of specific kinds of goods (including food, shelter, health care, information, and political participation) in order to flourish; that the most deprived should be given priority; and that poverty is a denial of human rights (CESCR 2001). It also asserts that equality and non-discrimination, including socio-economic equality, are not secondary, but central to realization of human rights (MacNaughton 2009).

We do not claim that attention to human rights provides the definitive, unquestionable answers to all economic policy questions. What such attention can help us do is to identify policies that are not consistent with obligations to realize human rights, and those that are. In choosing among policies which are consistent with human rights obligations, human rights analysis can also provide some guidance on the sequencing of policies (attention to the most deprived should have priority, because of the immediate obligation to ensure satisfaction of minimum essential levels) and on procedures (which must be transparent, participatory and accountable).

Notes

1   This chapter draws upon Balakrishnan and Elson 2008; Balakrishnan et al. 2011; and Balakrishnan and Elson 2011.
2   More information can be found on the human rights system on the website of the High Commission for Human Rights: www.ohcr.org.
3   It replaced the Commission on Human Rights. See www.ohchr.org/EN/HRBodies/HRC/Pages/AboutCouncil.aspx.
4   These guidelines appear in several publications. They are given in full as in Annex 5 of OHCHR 2005.
5   For instance, the Report of the High Commissioner for Human Rights (2002) focuses on trade in agriculture.
6   See further CESCR 2000, General Comment 14, para 54; CESCR 2003, General Comment 15, paras 16(a) and 48.
7   Obligations with respect to international development cooperation between governments are explicitly referred to in Article 2 of ICESCR, and underlined in specific provisions in Article 11 (right to an adequate standard of living). Articles 22 and 23 specifically refer to the need for international measures. In 1990 CESCR General Comment 3 stated that: "international co-operation for development ... is an obligation of all States." Further clarification of the meaning of maximum available resources by the CESCR included reference to development assistance, as noted above (CESCR 2007).

References

Alston, P. (2015a) *Report of Special Rapporteur on Extreme Poverty and Human Rights on the World Bank*. UN Document A/70/274.

Alston, P. (2015b) *Tax Policy Is Human Rights Policy: The Irish Debate*. Keynote Address at Christian Aid conference on The Human Rights Impact of Tax and Fiscal Policy, Dublin, 12 February 2015.

Balakrishnan, R. and Elson, D. (2008). Auditing economic policy in the light of obligations on economic and social rights. *Essex Human Rights Review* (5)1, pp. 1–19.

Balakrishnan, R. and Elson, D. (2011). Introduction. In: R. Balakrishnan and D. Elson, eds., *Economic Policy and Human Rights: Holding Governments to Account*. London: Zed Books, pp. 1–27.

Balakrishnan, R., Elson, D., Heintz, J., and Lusiani, N. (2011). *Maximum Available Resources & Human Rights: Analytical Report*. New Brunswick: Center for Women's Global Leadership, Rutgers University. Available at: http://www.cwgl.rutgers.edu/docman/economic-and-social-rights-publications/362-maximumavailableresources-pdf/file [Accessed 11 Sept. 2015].

Committee on Economic, Social and Cultural Rights (CESCR). (1990). General Comment No. 3: The nature of States parties' obligations of the Covenant. (Art.2. para 1). Available at: http://tbinternet.ohchr.org/_layouts/treatybodyexternal/Download.aspx?symbolno=INT%2fCESCR%2fGEC%2f4758&Lang=en [Accessed 22 Sept. 2015].

Committee on Economic, Social and Cultural Rights (CESCR). (1999a). General Comment No. 11: Plans of action for primary education (Art.14). E/C.12/1994/4. Available at: http://tbinternet.ohchr.org/_layouts/treatybodyexternal/Download.aspx?symbolno=E%2fC.12%2f1999%2f4&Lang=en [Accessed 22 Sept. 2015].

Committee on Economic, Social and Cultural Rights (CESCR). (1999b). General Comment No. 12: The right to adequate food (Art.11). E/C.12/1999/5. Available at: http://tbinternet.ohchr.org/_layouts/treatybodyexternal/Download.aspx ?symbolno=E%2fC.12%2f1999%2f5&Lang=en [Accessed 22 Sept. 2015].

Committee on Economic, Social and Cultural Rights (CESCR). (1999c). General Comment No. 13: The right to education (article 13 of the Covenant). E/C.12/1999/10. Available at: http://tbinternet.ohchr.org/_layouts/ treatybodyexternal/Download.aspx?symbolno=E%2fC.12%2f1999%2f10&Lan g=en [Accessed 22 Sept. 2015].

Committee on Economic, Social and Cultural Rights (CESCR). (2000). General Comment No. 14: The right to the highest attainable standard of health, E/C.12/2000/4. Available at: http://tbinternet.ohchr.org/_layouts/treaty bodyexternal/Download.aspx?symbolno=E%2fC.12%2f2000%2f4&Lang=en [Accessed 22 Sept. 2015].

Committee on Economic, Social and Cultural Rights (CESCR). (2001). Substantive Issues Arising in the Implementation of the International Covenant on Economic, Social and Cultural Rights: Poverty and the International Covenant on Economic, Social and Cultural Rights, Statement adopted by the Committee on Economic, Social and Cultural Rights on 4 May 2001. E/C.12/2001/10. Available at: http://www2.ohchr.org/english/bodies/cescr/docs/state ments/E.C.12.2001.10Poverty-2001.pdf [Accessed 22 Sept. 2015].

Committee on Economic, Social and Cultural Rights (CESCR). (2003). General Comment No. 15: The right to water. E/C.12/2002/11. Available at: http:// tbinternet.ohchr.org/_layouts/treatybodyexternal/Download.aspx?symbolno =E%2fC.12%2f2002%2f11&Lang=en [Accessed 22 Sept. 2015].

Committee on Economic, Social and Cultural Rights (CESCR). (2005). General Comment No. 16: The equal right of men and women to the enjoyment of all economic, social and cultural rights (art. 3 of the International Covenant on Economic, Social and Cultural Rights). E/C.12/2005/4. Available at: http:// tbinternet.ohchr.org/_layouts/treatybodyexternal/Download.aspx?symbolno =E%2fC.12%2f2005%2f4&Lang=en [Accessed 22 Sept. 2015].

Committee on Economic, Social and Cultural Rights (CESCR). (2007). An Evaluation of the Obligation to Take Steps to the "Maximum of Available Resources" under an Optional Protocol to the Covenant. E/C.12/2007/1. Available at: http://daccess-dds-ny.un.org/doc/UNDOC/GEN/G07/441/ 63/PDF/G0744163.pdf?OpenElement [Accessed 26 Sept. 2015].

Convention on the Elimination of All Forms of Discrimination against Women (CEDAW). (1979). UN Women. Available at: http://www.un.org/women watch/daw/cedaw/cedaw.htm [Accessed 26 Sept. 2015].

Convention on the Elimination of All Forms of Discrimination against Women (CEDAW). (2004). General Recommendation No. 25, on article 4, paragraph 1, of the Convention on the Elimination of All Forms of Discrimination against Women, on temporary special measures. Available at: http://www.un.org/ womenwatch/daw/cedaw/recommendations/General%20recommen dation%2025%20%28English%29.pdf [Accessed 26 Sept. 2015].

Convention on the Elimination of All Forms of Racial Discrimination (CERD). (1969). Office of the High Commissioner for Human Rights. Available at: http://www.ohchr.org/EN/ProfessionalInterest/Pages/CERD.aspx [Accessed 26 Sept. 2015].

Heintz, J. (2012). Central banks: Do they have human rights obligations? *Rightingfinance.org*. Available at: http://www.rightingfinance.org/?p=44 [Accessed 11 Sept. 2015].

Hertel, S. and Minkler, L. (2007). Economic rights: The terrain. In: S. Hertel and L. Minkler, eds., *Economic Rights: Conceptual, Measurement and Policy Issues.* Cambridge: Cambridge University Press, pp. 1–36.

International Covenant on Economic, Social and Cultural Rights (ICESCR). (1966). Office of the High Commissioner for Human Rights. Available at: http://www.ohchr.org/EN/ProfessionalInterest/Pages/CESCR.aspx [Accessed 26 Sept. 2015].

Limburg Principles on the Implementation of the International Covenant on Economic, Social and Cultural Rights. (1986). ESCR-Net. Available at: https://www.escr-net.org/docs/i/425445 [Accessed 26 Sept. 2015].

Maastricht Guidelines on Violations of Economic, Social and Cultural Rights. (1997). University of Minnesota, Human Rights Library. Available at: https://www1.umn.edu/humanrts/instree/Maastrichtguidelines_.html [Accessed 26 Sept. 2015].

Maastricht Principles on Extraterritorial Obligations of States in the area of Economic, Social and Cultural Rights. (2012). Available at: http://www.fian.org/fileadmin/media/publications/2012.02.29_-_Maastricht_Principles_on_Extraterritorial_Obligations.pdf [Accessed 26 Sept. 2015].

Maastricht University and International Commission of Jurists. (2011). Maastricht Principles on Extraterritorial Obligations of States in the area of Economic, Social and Cultural Rights. Available at: http://www.maastrichtuniversity.nl/web/Institutes/MaastrichtCentreForHumanRights/MaastrichtETOPrinciples.htm [Accessed 26 Sept. 2015].

MacNaughton, G. (2009). Untangling equality and non-discrimination to promote the right to health care for all. *Health and Human Rights* 11(2), pp. 47–62.

Office of High Commissioner for Human Rights (OHCHR). (2005). Economic, Social and Cultural Rights: Handbook for National Human Rights Institutions. Available at: http://www.ohchr.org/Documents/Publications/training12en.pdf [Accessed 9 March 2015].

Saiz, I. (2013) Resourcing Rights: Combating Tax Injustice from a Human Rights Perspective. In: Colin Harvey, Aoife Nolan, and Rory O'Connell, eds., *Human Rights and Public Finance: Budget Analysis and the Advancement of Economic and Social Rights.* Oxford: Hart Publishing, pp. 77–106.

Tomasevskï, K. (1998). *Background Paper Submitted by Special Rapporteur on the Right to Education, Committee on Economic, Social and Cultural Rights.* 19th Session (E/C.12/1998/18).

Tomasevskï, K. (2005). Not education for all, only for those who can pay: The World Bank's model for financing primary education. *Law, Social Justice and Global Development Journal.* (1). Available at: www2.warwick.ac.uk/fac/soc/law/elj/lgd/2005_1/tomasevski/ [Accessed 11 Sept. 2015].

UNDP. (2010). The fiscal space challenge and financing for MDG achievements. In: *Beyond the Midpoint: Achieving the Millennium Development Goals.* New York: UNDP, pp. 76–87. Available at: http://www.uncdf.org/gfld/docs/midpoint-mdg.pdf [Accessed 26 Sept. 2015].

UNDRD. (1986). *Declaration on the Right to Development.* Resolution adopted by the General Assembly, 4 December, A/RES/41/128.

United Nations. (1993). *Vienna Declaration and Programme of Action*. A/CONF.157/23. Available at: http://www.ohchr.org/Documents/Professional Interest/vienna.pdf [Accessed 26 Sept. 2015].

3 What does inequality have to do with human rights?

The realization of human rights cannot be separated from broader questions of economic and social justice. Global financial and economic crises, armed conflict and militarism, dangers to public health, gender-based and other forms of violence, food insecurity and climate change have intensified vulnerabilities and have threatened the realization of rights. Within this constellation of factors affecting the realization of rights, inequality in income and wealth has emerged globally as an area of growing concern. The human rights framework has started to engage with the question of inequalities in income and wealth, offering partial guidance on the implications of increasingly polarized societies and what obligations governments have to address this issue. Given the rise in inequality, it is critical to more fully understand the connections between realization of human rights and inequality.

This chapter explores the relationship between human rights and inequalities in income and wealth. It begins with a consideration of different approaches to understanding inequality—with a specific critique of the approach of the economic theories that dominate current policy discourse. The mainstream economics approach is then contrasted with one based in the human rights framework. The chapter then turns to the question of how income and wealth inequality affects realized outcomes with regard to the enjoyment of specific rights. The chapter considers how the distribution of resources affects political dynamics and power relations within which specific rights are realized. Pulling this analysis together, it concludes with a summary of the impact of inequality on human rights and what the human rights framework has to say about the distribution of income and wealth in society.

Current levels of inequality are extreme and, in many countries around the world, there has been an upward trend in income and wealth inequality since the 1980s (UNDP 2013). A 2014 study found that nearly half of the world's wealth was owned by just one percent of the population, and the wealth of the richest one percent amounted to $110 trillion, or about 65 times that of the bottom half (Fuentes-Nieva 2014). One measure of inequality is the Gini coefficient. The Gini coefficient is a number between

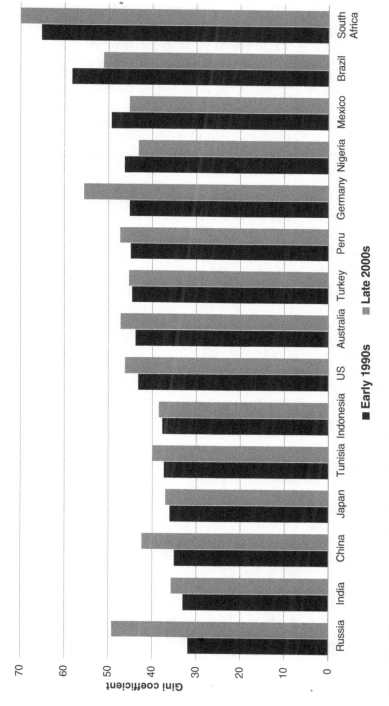

Figure 3.1 Changes in income distribution from the early 1990s to the late 2000s (Gini coefficient, income before taxes and subsidies) Estimates from UNDP (2013)

zero and one that would take on a value of one if all income were held by a single person and a value of zero if income were shared equally. A larger Gini coefficient, therefore, indicates greater inequality. Figure 3.1 shows that, within many countries in a range of distinct regions, the Gini coefficient has increased from the early 1990s to the late 2000s—indicating worsening inequalities. Among the countries shown in Figure 3.1 only Brazil, Mexico, and Nigeria show a decline in inequality.[1] Elsewhere, inequality has intensified.

The extent of income and wealth inequality at both the national and global levels has potentially important implications for the realization of human rights. But equally important, expanding inequalities raise important questions of what is fair and just. The human rights framework, as one approach to evaluating economic and social outcomes with regard to social justice, must engage with the question of inequality—how much, if any, inequality is acceptable, and what limits does growing inequality place on the fulfillment of basic rights?

Approaches to understanding inequality

When people speak of inequality, they often have in mind an unequal distribution of income or wealth. However, people experience inequalities across a number of dimensions. There are inequalities in educational attainment, in health, and in the distribution of power. The free time men and women have is unequally distributed, once all demands for work, both paid work on the job and unpaid work at home, are taken into account. Inequalities in income and wealth are associated with other disparities. For instance, low-income households have worse health outcomes on average (Subramanian and Kawachi 2004). Furthermore, inequalities can be measured with respect to different units of society— between individuals, between households, between social groups (e.g. race, gender, and ethnicity), and between countries. The emphasis in this chapter is on inequalities in income and wealth between individuals, households, social groups, and countries—and the relationship of these inequalities to human rights.

Inequality can be defined in various ways and the generic term "inequality" actually reflects a range of distinct inequalities. One important distinction is between "horizontal inequality" and "vertical inequality." Horizontal inequality is defined as inequality between culturally defined or socially constructed groups. Inequalities with respect to gender, race, ethnicity, religion, caste, and sexuality are all examples of horizontal inequalities. Vertical inequality refers to inequality between individuals or between households. The overall income or wealth distribution of an economy reflects vertical inequality, as do commonly used measurements of inequality, such as the Gini coefficient. The distinction between horizontal and vertical inequality is particularly salient when considering the human rights framework, since the issues around horizontal inequality are much more developed in discussions of economic and social rights than are issues around vertical inequality.

There are many approaches to analyzing and assessing the impact of inequalities, with the human rights framework representing just one tradition. In economics, the dominant approach has been neoclassical economics, which is a theoretical framework used to explain the determination of prices, decisions over production and consumption, and the distribution of income. Individual rational choice constitutes the core of neoclassical theory—each firm makes choices to maximize its own profits, and individuals or households maximize their own "utility," that is, the satisfaction they get from their consumption decisions. Although neoclassical economics has a theory of what determines income distribution based on the productivity of labor, capital, and other factors of production, it sidesteps the question of the consequences of inequality and instead evaluates economic outcomes primarily in terms of efficiency. Given the dominance of neoclassical theory in evaluating and analyzing economic outcomes, it is worth examining the relationship between this approach and inequality in some detail. We will then look at how the human rights framework incorporates issues of inequality.

In neoclassical theory, the distribution of assets, individual preferences, and technology are all taken as given. From this starting point, production takes place, consumers make choices, and markets coordinate exchanges. If markets remain unfettered and individuals can choose freely, according to the theory, the end result will be an efficient allocation of the goods and services produced in the economy. What does "efficient" mean? In this case, it means that no one can be made better off without making someone else worse off—a concept referred to as "Pareto efficiency" after the Italian economist Vilfredo Pareto, who wrote in the nineteenth and early twentieth centuries. Note that the idea of Pareto efficiency says nothing about income or wealth inequality. You could have a very unequal society that is also efficient in the Pareto sense.

One practical application of the idea of Pareto efficiency is the use of cost-benefit analysis to evaluate policy choices. Cost-benefit analysis measures the costs and benefits of implementing a particular policy—if the benefits are greater than the costs, the policy should be adopted. The concept of Pareto efficiency is used to justify this approach. If those who benefit were to compensate those who lose (i.e. those who pay the costs) of a particular policy, the winners could fully compensate the losers, making some better off without making anyone worse off—i.e. the definition of an improvement in Pareto efficiency.[2] Such compensation hardly ever takes place. Therefore, in practice, cost-benefit analysis ignores the distributive consequences of policy choices. The rich could receive all the benefits of a particular policy, and it would still be deemed a social improvement as long as the benefits outweigh the costs.

Within the neoclassical framework, the distribution of wealth—who owns what assets—is determined prior to economic production, market exchange, and income generation, with incomes coming from wages paid and profits earned. In an efficient economy, the technical character of production determines the distribution of income. Wages are assumed to be determined by the productivity of labor and profits from the productivity of capital. Therefore, the question of what is a just distribution of income and wealth falls outside of the purview of economic theory. Neoclassical thinking is largely silent on questions of inequality and instead focuses on defining the conditions under which an efficient allocation of resources emerges, taking some of the most important factors that determine well-being as being determined prior to production, consumption, and exchange.

Preferences also have a major role to play. Neoclassical economics assumes that preferences are given and that the order of preferences defines individual measurements of well-being. In other words, a person may prefer A to B and B to C. Given this information, a number can be assigned to A, B, and C that preserves this ordering (A is better/greater than B, which is better/greater than C). This number—called "utility"—is interpreted as an indicator of individual well-being. The exact value assigned to utility is arbitrary as long as the numbers preserve the preference ordering. But there is a catch—since the numerical value of utility is arbitrary, standard neoclassical theory assumes that the value of utility cannot be compared across individuals. Under the solution to the neoclassical model, all individuals are achieving the highest possible utility (remember: with a given set of preferences, asset distribution, and technologies). However, we cannot say whether any single person is "happier" than any other person. Utility is purely subjective in the sense that people have arbitrary preferences that cannot be compared.

This assumption effectively rules out any consideration of inequality in a social assessment of well-being (Sen 1992). Why? According to the theory, the poorest person in society will maximize utility, as will the richest person. But we cannot say that the poorest person is any less happy or satisfied than the richest person, because utilities cannot be compared across individuals. Since utilities are subjective, the rich could be miserable in the midst of their abundance while the poor are blissfully content with what little they have. All we can say is that everyone is as happy as they, as individuals, could possibly be, given their preferences, their assets, and the available technology.

Variations on neoclassical theory attempt to get around this problem by introducing a "taste" for equality (Alesina and Giuliano 2009). Individuals still maximize their own utility, but with this twist, they can have preferences for redistribution based on their subjective assessment of how other people are doing. But this does not get us very far. These tastes are still given and fixed. If we follow this line of thinking, the acceptable level of inequality is once again determined by the arbitrary factor of taste.

However, there is growing concern about what is an acceptable level of inequality in society. It is generally agreed that inequalities are important to take into account when deciding whether societies are just or fair, but neoclassical economic theory does not seriously contend with the question of inequality. Values about inequality and redistribution are not simply about an individual's current position in the economy, with poorer households more critical about an unequal distribution of resources. A number of factors shape these values: culture, personal history, family, education, social norms, and perceptions of economic mobility, among others. This indicates that people routinely make interpersonal comparisons of well-being, and these comparisons are central for assessing the fairness of a situation. Unlike neoclassical economics, any framework for social justice which features concern over inequality must allow for some comparison of well-being across individuals. Inequality raises the consideration of welfare to the social level. Instead of using a concept based on a narrow idea of individual satisfaction or prescribed tastes, comparisons of well-being between individuals and between groups allow us to consider the issue of fairness.

In considering questions of fairness and justice, a distinction is often made between equality of opportunity and equality of outcome. Equality of opportunity typically means that all people are treated identically, for instance, in the application of the law, when making employment or credit decisions, or in determining access to education or health care. The idea of equality of opportunity is closely linked to the concept of meritocracy and is perfectly consistent with inequalities in income and wealth outcomes. It typically assumes that societies will be stratified—with some people occupying more privileged positions than others.

In this situation, there must be a mechanism for allocating the better social and economic positions to individuals in a way that is fair and unbiased. If there is equality of opportunity, then equivalently qualified individuals will have the same chance of securing a favorable position in society and will not be excluded on the basis of arbitrary criteria such as gender, race, or the socio-economic standing of their parents. Equality of opportunity stresses that people should have similar choices available to them, although they may have different talents, skills, and abilities that make them more suited to certain pursuits than others. If equality of opportunities is secured, then inequalities in income and wealth are a result of the choices people make and the endowments they happen to have as individuals.

In contrast, fairness and social justice can be defined in terms of realized outcomes. Realized outcomes can be measured along a number of dimensions: income, wealth, health, education, etc. Depending on how equality of outcome is defined, it may or may not imply equality of financial resources. For example, someone with a chronic illness or disability may require greater medical expenditures to have similar well-being outcomes to those of a person without these health challenges. Equalizing health outcomes does not imply that the resources used to access health services are equally distributed.

John Rawls developed a particular approach to social justice based on realized outcomes, linked to freedom of choice. In deriving his arguments, he used a concept called the "veil of ignorance" (Rawls 1971). Imagine that you are free to choose the society in which you will live, including the degree of inequality in that society. The only catch is that you do not know which social position you will occupy. In the case of income inequality, you have the same chance of being the richest person as being the poorest. Rawls argued that people would choose the society in which the poorest (or least well-off) were in the best possible position that could be achieved. Notice that this does not imply equality of outcome. Some individuals may occupy a more privileged position, but only if, by granting them a better place in society, they improve outcomes that make the poorest better off. For example, some people may become higher paid doctors or engineers who, through their education and skills, generate social benefits that help the least advantaged.

Rawlsian approaches to social justice emphasize the importance of individual freedoms, for example, asking the question of which society people would freely choose, if they had the opportunity to do so. The capabilities approach, pioneered by Amartya Sen (1980), also emphasizes individual freedoms. It conceptualizes individual well-being, not in terms of levels of utility as in the neoclassical framework but in terms of substantive choices and opportunities, in terms of how far a person can do and be the things they have reason to value, such as being free from hunger and having the choice to take part in the life of the community. It poses well-being as inherently multidimensional and not reducible to a single dimension.

Looking deeper into these issues, it is often impossible to clearly separate equality of outcome from equality of opportunity. Suppose we extend the concept of equality of opportunity to mean that individuals should have similar choices in the course of their lives—in other words, equality of opportunity can be framed in terms of the concept of capabilities (Sen 2009). However, people will not have similar choices if they lack the income needed to pursue those choices, if they die prematurely from a preventable illness, or if they are shut out of educational opportunities.

The human rights framework has at its core the principles of non-discrimination and equality. According to the non-discrimination principle, the realization of rights should not differ across individuals based on gender, race, ethnicity, nationality, or other social grouping—in other words, there is a strong emphasis on horizontal equality in the human rights framework. People should also have equal opportunity to claim their rights—i.e. human rights principles should apply to all persons equally. Note that this does not necessarily imply a perfectly equal distribution of income and wealth. The distribution of resources in society consistent with a human rights approach would be one that guarantees that individuals have an equal enjoyment of the realization of their basic rights without discriminatory outcomes. We discuss the implications of what this means later in the chapter.

The term "equality" in the expression "non-discrimination and equality" is often interpreted to refer to formal legal equality, meaning that all people are equal before the law—that is, the laws apply to all people and should be applied by the courts equally to all. But the Universal Declaration of Human Rights also stresses that people enjoy "equal protection of the law"—implying that the laws themselves should provide for equal treatment, that states must extend the same rights and privileges to all citizens. Within the human rights framework, this implies that the government must treat all people equally when it takes steps to ensure that rights are protected, respected and fulfilled.

Moreover, subsequent clarifications by human rights treaty bodies have made it clear that non-discrimination and equality also refers to substantive equality (CESCR 2005, General Comment 16). Human rights look beyond equality of treatment and opportunity, and embrace the idea of substantive equality. This approach recognizes that there are structural sources of inequality and indirect forms of discrimination. Therefore, equality has to be understood in relation to outcomes and results in addition to opportunities and conduct. If we focus on equality of outcomes, different treatment might be required to achieve realized equality of outcomes in many cases.

Before turning to the question of how inequality in income and wealth affects the realization of human rights, it is helpful to briefly consider the question of poverty and its relationship to the issues discussed here. Inequality in income and wealth is related to the concept of poverty, defined in terms of income or consumption, but the two are distinct concepts. Measurements of poverty focus on the lower end of the income distribution and therefore provide a partial and incomplete picture of the entire distribution of income. Poverty is a measure of deprivation, not of distribution. The poverty threshold is typically defined by the income or expenditures required for a household to purchase a minimum basket of consumption goods and services. If income or consumption expenditures fall below this threshold, the members of that household are considered to be poor. Lower rates of poverty do not necessarily imply less inequality. Poverty declines when the incomes of poor households increase, but inequality can still worsen if the incomes of the well-off grow even faster.

International comparisons of poverty rates are difficult because the nature of deprivation is often context-specific and different countries utilize different definitions of poverty. The World Bank uses a poverty line of $1.25 per person per day, adjusted for price differences, to generate international estimates of poverty. However, this poverty line is quite arbitrary and therefore has serious shortcomings.[3] For example, the $1.25 per day threshold is not appropriate for measuring poverty in high-income countries, since most households in these countries that are clearly poor will have incomes that exceed this international cutoff. Even among developing economies, being below the $1.25 threshold will have different meanings from one country to the next.

Not all concepts of poverty use an absolute threshold, below which a household is considered to be poor. In the European Union, the poverty line is typically set at 60 percent of median equivalized household income.[4] This approach to measuring poverty reflects the concept of "relative poverty". Relative poverty is defined in relation to the median standard of living. Specifically, the relative poverty line is often defined as some fraction of median income. Concepts of relative poverty have the advantage of recognizing that needs are socially determined and that deprivation is experienced in relation to the typical standard of living in a society. It means that the poverty line, in terms of real income, goes up when real median income rises. But this also means that the poverty line falls when real median income falls. Because relative poverty is defined relative to median living standards, it is more directly related to measurements of inequality. When relative poverty increases, income inequality must have increased, at least in the lower half of the income distribution.

The issue of income poverty has been investigated by the former Independent Expert/Special Rapporteur on Human Rights and Extreme Poverty, Magdalena Sepúlveda Carmona. In a report on her mission to Ireland in 2011, she used an expansive understanding of extreme poverty in line with concepts of relative poverty. She noted that:

> Different countries have different levels of resources and their different circumstances must be taken into account when assessing efforts to combat existing levels of poverty and social exclusion. To assess compliance with economic, social and cultural rights obligations, the level of scrutiny for developed States, such as Ireland, is higher than for middle-income or low-income countries.
>
> (Carmona 2011)

She based her assessment on the concept of poverty used by the government of Ireland:

> People are living in poverty if their incomes and resources (material, cultural, and social) are so inadequate as to preclude them from having a standard of living which is regarded as acceptable by Irish society generally.
>
> (Ibid.)

The United Nations Committee on Economic, Social and Cultural Rights has adopted an approach similar to the capabilities approach and stressed that governments have an obligation to secure minimum core levels of the fulfillment of economic and social rights. In this approach, deprivation is defined with regard to the specific right in question, rather than a level of income—e.g. housing, food, health, or social security. As discussed in Chapter 2, the Committee clarifies what is meant by minimum core levels with regard to the International Covenant on Economic, Social and Cultural Rights (ICESCR):

> A minimum core obligation to ensure the satisfaction of, at the very least, minimum essential levels of each of the rights is incumbent upon every State party. Thus, for example, a State party in which any significant number of individuals is deprived of essential foodstuffs, of essential primary healthcare, of basic shelter and housing, or of the most basic forms of education is, prima facie, failing to discharge its obligations under the Covenant.
>
> (CESCR 1990, General Comment 3)

The Human Rights Council has agreed that the human rights approach imposes conditions on prioritization in policy-making to protect poor people against trade-offs that may be harmful to them, especially trade-offs that lead to retrogression from existing levels of realization of human rights or lead to non-fulfillment of these minimum core obligations (OHCHR 2012).

However, our goal here is to look beyond the issue of minimum core levels, and explore the implications of inequality for the realization of rights. The extent of inequality matters to human rights—specifically with regard to inequalities in the realization of specific rights. When it comes to the question of inequalities in income and wealth, the human rights framework, as it is currently interpreted, is less precise in defining obligations than in relation to other dimensions of inequality (MacNaughton 2013). In part, this is because income and wealth are means to an end, not the end itself. Having a certain level of income helps people realize their rights—to health, education, housing, an adequate standard of living, and so forth. But it is the rights, taken together, that are important, rather than the precise channel through which they are realized. What we need to look at is how inequality in income and wealth affects the realization of rights and what should be done about it.

Inequality in income and wealth and the realization of rights

Income and wealth inequality have a direct impact on the realization of certain rights. Inequality is often associated with poorer outcomes with regard to health, education, and other economic and social rights (Wilkinson and Pickett 2009). It is not surprising that richer households enjoy better outcomes than poorer ones. However, inequality itself can lead to worse outcomes—even controlling for the level of income. Put another way, low-income households in a very unequal society may do worse than households with the identical income in a more equal society (Ibid.). In this section we will focus on rights to education, health, housing, and a life free from violence to show the links between inequality and the realization of rights.

The Universal Declaration of Human Rights (1948) states that everyone has the right to education and that education should be free at least at the elementary level. Studies have shown that greater income inequality is associated with lower educational achievement (UNDP 2013). One significant factor determining access to education and unequal educational outcomes is the allocation of government spending. Income inequality partly determines inequality in access to education, but access also depends on how public resources for education are distributed. Poorer communities can have strong schools if there is public support for quality education. Unequal educational access and outcomes potentially have a long-term impact on the realization of other rights in that there may be "opportunity hoarding." Opportunity hoarding refers to "the process through which disparities become permanent. This occurs when certain defined groups take control of valuable resources and assets for their benefit and 'seek to secure rewards from sequestered resources.' And this might be different types of resources such as public expenditure, access to quality education, or profitable jobs" (Fuentes-Nieva 2014, p. 20). We discuss these political dynamics later in the chapter.

Article 12 of the International Covenant on Economic, Social and Cultural Rights (1966) recognizes "the right of everyone to the enjoyment of the highest attainable standard of physical and mental health." Countries with higher levels of income inequality have worse health outcomes—in terms of key indicators, such as life expectancy—compared to other countries with similar levels of GDP (Wilkinson and Pickett 2009). Inequality affects children's health as well. Figure 3.2 shows a negative relationship between inequality—measured as the ratio of the income share of the top 10 percent of households to the share of the bottom 10 percent—and the rate of under-5 child mortality among a group of higher income countries.[5] Greater inequality is associated with higher rates of child mortality among countries at similar levels of development.

With regard to the impact of inequality on housing, an increase in inequality can affect the availability of housing for lower income households. In the United States, for example, studies have shown that when there is a limited or relatively unresponsive supply of housing, there is a direct link between the increasing inequality and the price of housing (Matlack and Vigor 2008). This has an adverse impact on a poorer household's ability to secure housing and lowers the income they have at their disposal once housing costs are paid (Ibid.).

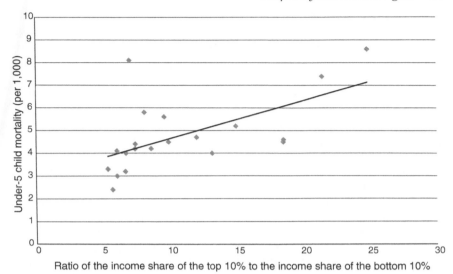

Figure 3.2 Income inequality and under-5 child mortality, high income countries, 2010
World Bank (2010) (Note: Figures for Chile are for 2011)

Inequality has macroeconomic implications in terms of its effect on growth and economic performance. Although the effect of inequality on growth does not directly undermine rights, slower rates of economic growth limit the resources available for the progressive realization of rights. However, the relationship between growth, inequality, and human rights is complex. Some statistical analysis has shown that greater inequality leads to slower growth (Cingano 2014). There are several reasons for this relationship. As discussed earlier, inequality can reduce educational attainment, thereby lowering growth. Greater inequality may also affect total levels of consumption by reducing the purchasing power of households in the lower end of the income distribution, thus reducing demand and growth since lower income households tend to consume a larger portion of their total income than do richer ones (Stiglitz 2012).

However, other studies have shown that greater inequality can be associated with faster growth if increased inequality supports profitability and investment. For example, the apartheid system in South Africa institutionalized inequalities between blacks and whites, creating conditions for higher rates of investment and growth, particularly in the 1950s and 1960s, by ensuring the availability of a large pool of inexpensive labor that supported high rates of profitability (Heintz 2009). Similarly, studies have shown that a larger gap between women's and men's wages is associated with faster growth and increased exports in specific emerging market economies in Asia, Europe, and Latin America (Seguino 2000). A larger gender wage gap means that women's paid labor is relatively cheaper than men's, again providing a pool of inexpensive, productive labor. In these examples, violations of the human rights principle of non-discrimination actually support faster rates of growth.

Inequality affects economic stability and has been a contributing factor to economic crises, such as the 2008 global financial crisis (Rajan 2011). Financial and economic crises are bad for the realization of rights and lead to high rates of unemployment, loss of homeownership, cutbacks to government spending, and reductions in living standards. The poor are more vulnerable to the negative effects of crises and have fewer resources at their disposal to weather a severe downturn. This implies that economic volatility can further worsen inequalities—in both income and the enjoyment of rights (Stiglitz 2012). Therefore, economic instability represents another channel through which inequality affects the enjoyment of rights.

Increased inequality can impact tax revenue—and this affects the resources available to governments to support the realization of rights. For example, the share of wealth in India held by the country's billionaires has gone from 1.8 percent in 2003 to 26 percent by 2008. During this period, the tax structure changed, reducing the ratio of tax revenue to GDP (Fuentes-Nieva 2014). In India, there has been an increase in corruption and tax loopholes, and a great amount of the wealth is hidden through shell companies, and changes in the tax law have affected the ability of government to mobilize domestic resources (Ibid.). Similarly, in Pakistan, despite the sizeable net worth of parliamentarians, only a few pay taxes, with many paying no taxes at all (Ibid.). The increased concentration of wealth has had an impact on the tax code and structure, directly impacting the ability of the government to raise the maximum of available resources to fulfill rights.[6]

Political economy, inequality, and human rights

In the human rights framework, the state is the primary duty bearer and has the obligation to respect, protect, and fulfill rights. The realization of rights therefore depends on a functioning state that can be held to account. Democratic participation and transparency are also central to the realization of rights. People must have access to information and should be able to claim their rights by participating in political processes that ensure that the government meets its obligations and is responsive to the population's needs. Inequality in income and wealth impacts formal and informal political processes in ways that determine people's access to education, healthcare, jobs, and social security.

However, some political scientists argue that a democratic process is able to offset the impact of inequalities in income and wealth. The "median voter theorem" suggests there will be pressures for redistribution in unequal societies (Alesina and Rodrik 1994). How does this theory work?

Imagine that you are living in a democratic system in which the majority of the population gets to decide which economic policy the government follows. In this example, the median voter is the person who is exactly in the middle of the income (or wealth) distribution—half the population has the same or less income (or wealth) as the median voter. Increasing inequality concentrates income and wealth in the hands of those people at the upper end of the distribution. The gap in income (or wealth) between the top end of the distribution and the bottom half of the distribution widens. As this gap grows, support for redistributive policies among those in the bottom half gains strength. Since the majority of the population decides on economic policy, the government will implement policies that redistribute income and wealth.

Under this form of the median voter theorem, inequality in income and wealth is not necessarily a problem, since a democratic political process automatically adjusts for these imbalances. For economic and social rights, this would imply that growing inequality would be met by increasing political pressures on the state to ensure that the rights of the majority are secure. This approach makes very strong demands on the robustness of the political system. It assumes that people are able to claim their rights, that the state is democratically accountable, that the policies supported by the majority do not undermine the rights of other groups (racial, ethnic, cultural, etc.), that global integration places no limits on the policy choices of national governments, and that elite economic interests are not able to unduly influence economic policy. However, inequality in income and wealth engenders inequality in the distribution of power in society, and this undermines the pure form of the median voter theorem (Stiglitz 2012). When the political power of the elites expands as the income and wealth distribution becomes more polarized, this compromises the realization of human rights—economic and social rights as well as civil and political rights. There is significant evidence that supports the idea that greater inequality reinforces political processes that compromise the realization of economic and social rights. As Philip Alston, Special Rapporteur on Extreme Poverty, stated in his 2015 report: "Economic inequalities seem to encourage political capture and the unequal realization of civil and political rights" (UN Human Rights Council 2015).

Economic elites are less likely to support policies that aim at securing the broad-based provision of health care, education, housing, and jobs when those policies are costly to those at the upper end of the distribution relative to the benefits they receive (Sokoloff and Zolt 2006). Studies that look at variations across a range of countries have shown that, contrary to the median voter theorem, greater inequality is associated with less redistributive government spending, as measured by expenditures on social security and welfare as a share of GDP (de Mello and Tiongson 2003). Similarly, there is evidence that social expenditures fall when the gap between the middle class (the median of the income distribution) and the top 10 percent widens

(Schwabish, Smeeding and Osberg 2004). Economic elites are likely to resist progressive forms of taxation, which limits the ability of the government to mobilize resources for the fulfillment of rights (Sokoloff and Zolt 2006).

Exploring these issues in greater depth, one research study on the political dynamics of the United States analyzed data on 1,779 policy cases between 1981 and 2002 for which survey data was available on whether the general public favored or opposed a proposed policy change. The study examined the impact of three variables on actual policy changes: (1) the average citizen's policy preferences, i.e. preferences at the median income; (2) the policy preferences of economic elites, measured as preferences at the ninetieth income percentile; and (3) the policy positions of interest groups. The researchers further distinguished between business and professional interest groups and those interest groups representing mass-based organizing. They found that economic elites and organized interest groups have significant influence on government policy, yet average citizens (i.e. the median voter) and mass-based interest groups have little or no independent impact (Gilens and Page 2014).

Inequality in income and wealth also affects the stability of the economic, social, and political environment with consequences for the fulfillment of rights. For example, inequality has been shown to be correlated with indicators of political violence, including state violence against citizens (Landman and Larizza 2009). As inequality becomes more severe, the gap between the haves and the have-nots widens, and conflicts over the distribution of income, wealth, and economic opportunities intensify. These conflicts may trigger widespread social and political instability. When democratic accountability is limited, it is more likely that distributive conflicts will be contained through state repression that undermines basic rights.

Laura Ramirez Takeuschi (2014) has shown that conflict arises when the level of inequality threatens social trust. Furthermore, chances of violence increase when income inequality between households (vertical inequality) and intergroup inequality (horizontal inequality) is very high. The Universal Declaration of Human Rights (1948) states that "everyone has the right to life, liberty and security of person." Violent conflict undermines these basic human rights (Takeuschi 2014).

Inequality between countries and the right to development

Up to this point, much of the discussion in this chapter has focused on inequality within a particular country or economy. However, inequality at the global level is also a human rights issue. Taking a global view, changes in inequality are due to two factors: a widening or narrowing of the gaps that exist between the households within countries and positive or negative shifts in the extent of inequality between countries. It is this second dimension that we focus on here.

The United Nations Declaration on the Right to Development, adopted in 1986, is the human rights document that comes closest to directly addressing inequalities between countries. This is partly because the way "development" is conceived in the Declaration is as a collective process rather than a specific individual right. Therefore, the Declaration emphasizes both rights at the national level and rights at the individual level. The preamble to the Declaration (1986) states

> Development is a comprehensive economic, social, cultural and political process, which aims at the constant improvement of the well-being of the entire population and of all individuals on the basis of their active, free and meaningful participation in development and in the fair distribution of benefits resulting therefrom ...

Distribution is clearly a central concern of the Declaration, both at the country and individual level. The distribution of benefits reflects an outcome of the process of development, including government policies that support the realization of rights. However, the Right to Development also emphasizes equality of opportunity at the collective level:

> The right to development is an inalienable human right and that equality of opportunity for development is a prerogative both of nations and of individuals who make up nations ...

The issues surrounding global inequalities impinge on various dimensions of the Right to Development. Though there has always been inequality between countries, policy changes, particularly in the governance of international trade and finance, have taken on a new dimension in which global inequalities become legally sanctioned at the international level and represent a particular structure of the global economy. As discussed in greater depth in Chapters 6 and 7, the current structures of global economic governance are shaped by the vested interests of elites throughout the world and in the national interests of the richest countries. In international financial institutions, such as the World Bank and the IMF, countries receive votes based on their shares in these institutions. These institutions have significant influence on the policies that developing countries adopt, and these policies may hinder the realization of human rights (Solomon 2007). The economic dynamism of countries such as India and China has affected the global balance of power, but decisions that are made at the global level remain the purview of a handful of influential countries—such as those represented in the G20.

Bilateral and multilateral trade negotiations provide an example of these dynamics, often limiting the policy choices available to governments for the realization of human rights. For example, agreements on trade in services, such as those reflected in the General Agreement on Trade in

Services (GATS) and provisions regarding intellectual property rights, as reflected in the Agreement on Trade-Related Aspects of Intellectual Property Rights (TRIPS) could affect governments' ability to pursue policies that support the right to education and the right to health (Verger and van Paassen 2012). The decisions to open up trade in education works in favor of those countries that have the capacity to export educational services and diminishes the ability of other countries to legislate their educational systems (Ibid.). With regard to health, intellectual property rights provisions protect the interests of pharmaceutical companies, which are mostly located in high-income countries and often undermine efforts to provide low-cost medicine to people who need it. The processes whereby these trade agreements are negotiated are characterized by unequal power relations at the global level, which is linked to inequalities between countries (Ibid.).

Global inequalities also affect a country's ability to implement independent macroeconomic policies that affect the realization of rights through their impact on maximum available resources—such as the revenue available to finance government spending, the latitude to pursue goals such as improving employment outcomes, or managing important prices such as the exchange rate. More powerful economies have a wider range of policy options available when responding to economic shocks compared to smaller, more dependent economies (Ocampo and Vos 2008). These global inequalities in policy space are discussed in depth in Chapter 7.

The International Covenant on Economic, Social and Cultural Rights (ICESCR) recognizes that a country has obligations with regard to the realization of economic and social rights beyond its borders—often referred to as extraterritorial obligations.[7] Specifically, Article 2, para 1 of ICESCR states that states should "take steps, individually and through international assistance and cooperation, especially economic and technical, to the maximum of its available resources, with a view to achieving progressively the full realization of the rights recognized in the present Covenant by all appropriate means" (ICESCR 1966, Article 2, para 1). Article 2, para 1 suggests that better-resourced countries have an obligation to assist poorer countries. In other words, countries in more privileged positions should support the realization of economic and social rights elsewhere in the face of global inequalities. The Committee on Economic, Social and Cultural Rights further emphasizes this commitment in its General Comment 3 (1990, para 13) with regard to the principle of maximum available resources:

> The Committee notes that the phrase 'to the maximum of its available resources' was intended by the drafters of the Covenant to refer to both the resources existing within a State and those available from the international community through international cooperation and assistance.

While the ICESCR and the concept of extraterritorial obligations emphasize the need for coordination and cooperation, the UN Declaration on the Right to Development (1986) also places emphasis on national sovereignty:

> The human right to development also implies the full realization of the right of peoples to self-determination, which includes, subject to the relevant provisions of both International Covenants on Human Rights, the exercise of their inalienable right to full sovereignty over all their natural wealth and resources.

There is a potential tension between guaranteeing national sovereignty and pursuing the kind of international cooperation needed for the realization of rights in today's globalized economy (Rodrik 2012). For instance, uncoordinated, independent actions by individual states are consistent with preserving national sovereignty, but may undermine global cooperation. Similarly, true cooperation may require states to give up some degree of sovereignty to act in ways that promote the common good. Some balance between preserving sovereignty and promoting international coordination is needed. One approach would be to equalize the degree of sovereignty across nations in a way that is consistent with global cooperation. As the Declaration on the Right to Development (1986) states, there is a need "to promote a new international economic order based on sovereign equality, interdependence, mutual interest and cooperation among all States, as well as to encourage the observance and realization of human rights." In order to achieve this outcome, existing global inequalities would need to be addressed as would the structures of the global economy that maintain these inequalities over time.

Conclusion

This chapter has explored the relationship between human rights and inequalities in income and wealth, contrasting human rights with other theoretical approaches used to evaluate social outcomes, specifically neoclassical economics. Human rights provide partial guidance on the implications of widening inequalities within and between the countries of the world. For instance, the principle of non-discrimination is concerned with horizontal inequalities in conduct and outcomes—that is, inequalities between different social groups—with respect to the enjoyment of rights. Similarly, the Declaration on the Right to Development recognizes the importance of the inequalities that exist between countries that can impede the realization of rights. However, the human rights framework stops short of declaring a particular distribution of income or wealth as fair or just.

This is partly because human rights are about realized outcomes that shape the choices and freedoms people enjoy in the course of their lives (Sen 2004). In this context, income and wealth are means to an end, not the ends themselves. Therefore, a just distribution of income is one that allows for the fullest realization of rights possible that is consistent with the principles of non-discrimination and equality. As Chapter 1 stressed, Article 28 of the Universal Declaration of Human Rights states that "everyone is entitled to a social and international order in which the rights and freedoms set forth in this Declaration can be fully realized." The distribution of income and wealth, and the concomitant political dynamics associated with a particular level of inequality in society, represents an important dimension of this social and international order (MacNaughton 2013). Therefore, there is an implicit obligation within the human rights framework for states to consider the impact of inequality on the realization of rights and, where inequality impedes the realization of rights, to take steps to move towards a more just distribution of income.

Notes

1 In some countries, particularly those in Latin America, reductions in inequality are explained, in part, by redistributive policies, such as cash transfers. Others argue that, in Latin America, alternative approaches to macroeconomic policies also may have contributed. See UNDP (2013).
2 The idea that a policy could be judged as having an improvement in social welfare if the winners could hypothetically compensate the losers is sometimes referred to as the Kaldor-Hicks criterion, after economists Nicholas Kaldor and John Hicks.
3 For a critique of the dollar-a-day poverty measure see Reddy and Pogge (2010).
4 Formally known as the "at risk of poverty threshold." See http://eurostat.ec.europa.eu/statistics_explained/index.php/Mainpage. Incomes are measured after social transfers and adjusted via a process known as "equivalization" to take account of the idea that larger families need less income per head to reach the same living standards as smaller families, due to economies of scale in the purchase of some household goods and services.
5 The countries are Canada, Chile, Czech Republic, Denmark, Estonia, Finland, Germany, Greece, Iceland, Ireland, Israel, Italy, Netherlands, Norway, Poland, Slovak Republic, Slovenia, Spain, United Kingdom, and United States.
6 Article 2.1 of the International Covenant on Economic, Social and Cultural Rights (ICESCR) states that governments should "take steps, individually and through international assistance and co-operation, especially economic and technical, to the maximum of its available resources, with a view to achieving progressively the full realization of the rights recognized."
7 See, for example, Carmona (2006); Coomans and Kamminga (2004); and Coomans (2011).

References

Alesina, A. and Giuliano, P. (2009). *Preferences for Redistribution*, IZA discussion papers, No. 4056. http://nbn-resolving.de/urn:nbn:de:101:1-20090327233 [Accessed 26 Sept. 2015].
Alesina, A. and Rodrik, D. (1994). Distributive politics and economic growth. *Quarterly Journal of Economics* 109(2), pp. 465–90.

Carmona, M. S. (2006). Obligations of "international assistance and cooperation" in an optional protocol to the International Covenant on Economic, Social and Cultural Rights. *Netherlands Quarterly of Human Rights* 24, pp. 271–303.

Carmona, M. S. (2011). *Report of the Independent Expert on the Question of Human Rights and Extreme Poverty, Mission to Ireland, Human Rights Council*, A/HRC/17/34/Add 2. Available at: http://www2.ohchr.org/english/bodies/hrcouncil/docs/17session/A.HRC.17.34.Add.2_en.pdf [Accessed 26 Sept. 2015].

Cingano, F. (2014). *Trends in Income Inequality and its Impact on Economic Growth*, OECD Social, Employment and Migration Working Papers, No. 163, OECD Publishing. Available at: http://dx.doi.org/10.1787/5jxrjncwxv6j-en [Accessed 26 Sept. 2015].

Committee on Economic, Social and Cultural Rights (CESCR). (1990). General Comment No. 3: The nature of States parties' obligations of the Covenant. (Article 2, para 1). Available at: http://tbinternet.ohchr.org/_layouts/treatybodyexternal/Download.aspx?symbolno=INT%2fCESCR%2fGEC%2f4758&Lang=en [Accessed 26 Sept. 2015].

Committee on Economic, Social and Cultural Rights (CESCR). (2005). General Comment No. 16: The equal right of men and women to the enjoyment of all economic, social and cultural rights (Article 3 of the International Covenant on Economic, Social and Cultural Rights). E/C.12/2005/4. Available at: http://tbinternet.ohchr.org/_layouts/treatybodyexternal/Download.aspx?symbolno=E%2fC.12%2f2005%2f4&Lang=en [Accessed 22 Sept. 2015].

Coomans, F. (2011). The extraterritorial scope of the International Covenant on Economic, Social and Cultural Rights in the work of the United Nations Committee on Economic, Social and Cultural Rights. *Human Rights Law Review* 11, pp. 1–35.

Coomans, F. and Kamminga, M. T., eds. (2004). *Extraterritorial Application of Human Rights Treaties*. Antwerp-Oxford: Intersentia.

De Mello, L. and Tiongson, E. R. (2003). *Income Inequality and Redistributive Government Spending*. IMF Working Paper WP/03/14. International Monetary Fund, Washington DC.

Fuentes-Nieva, R. (2014). *Working for the Few: Political Capture and Economic Inequality.*178 Oxfam Briefing Paper.

Gilens, M. and Page, B. I. (2014). Testing theories of American politics: elites, interest groups, and average citizens. *Perspectives on Politics* 12(3), pp. 564–81.

Heintz, J. (2009). Social structures of accumulation in South Africa. In: D. Kotz, T. Macdonough, and M. Reich, eds., *Social Structures of Accumulation*. Cambridge: Cambridge University Press. pp. 267–85.

International Covenant on Economic, Social and Cultural Rights (ICESCR). (1966). Office of the High Commissioner for Human Rights. Available at: http://www.ohchr.org/EN/ProfessionalInterest/Pages/CESCR.aspx [Accessed 26 Sept. 2015].

Landman, T. and Larizza, M. (2009). Inequality and human rights: Who controls what, when, and how. *International Studies Quarterly* 53, pp. 715–36.

MacNaughton, G. (2013). Beyond a minimum threshold: The right to social equality. In: L. Minkler, ed., *The State of Economic and Social Human Rights: A Global Overview*. Cambridge: Cambridge University Press, pp. 271–305.

Matlack, J. and Vigor, J. (2008). Do rising tides lift all prices? Income inequality and housing affordability. *Journal of Housing Economics* 17(3), pp. 212–24.

Ocampo, J. A. and Vos, R. (2008). *Policy Space and the Changing Paradigm in Conducting Macroeconomic Policies in Developing Countries*. BIS Paper No. 36. Basel, Switzerland: Bank for International Settlements.

Office of High Commissioner for Human Rights (OHCHR). (2012). *Principles and Guidelines for a Human Rights Approach to Poverty Reduction Strategies, HR/PUB/06/12*. Geneva: OHCHR.

Rajan, R. (2011). *Fault Lines: How Hidden Fractures Still Threaten the World Economy*. Princeton: Princeton University Press.

Rawls, J. (1971). *A Theory of Justice*. Cambridge, MA: Belknap Press (Harvard University).

Reddy, S. G. and Pogge, T. (2010). How not to count the poor. In: S. Anand, P. Segal, and J. Stiglitz, eds., *Debates on the Measurement of Global Poverty*. Oxford: Oxford University Press, pp. 42–85.

Rodrik, D. (2012). *The Globalization Paradox: Democracy and the Future of the World Economy*. New York: W.W. Norton.

Schwabish, J., Smeeding, T., and Osberg, L. (2004). *Income Distribution and Social Expenditures: A Crossnational Perspective*. Paper prepared for the Russell Sage Foundation, New York, October 2004.

Seguino, S. (2000). Gender inequality and economic growth: A cross-country analysis. *World Development* 28(7), pp. 1211–30.

Sen, A. (1980). Equality of what? In: S. McMurrin, ed., *Tanner Lectures on Human Values, Vol.1*. Cambridge: Cambridge University Press, pp. 197–220.

Sen, A. (1992). *Inequality Reexamined*. Cambridge, MA: Harvard University Press.

Sen, A. (2004). Capabilities, lists and public reason: Continuing the conversation. *Feminist Economics* 10(3), pp. 77–80.

Sen, A. (2009). *The Idea of Justice*. New York: Penguin Books.

Sokoloff, K. L. and Zolt, E. M. (2006). Inequality and the evolution of institutions of taxation. Evidence from the economic history of the Americas on how inequality may influence tax institutions. *Tax Law Review* 59(2), pp. 167–242.

Solomon, M. (2007). *International Economic Governance and Human Rights Accountability*. London School of Economics, Society and Economy Working Papers 9/2007.

Stiglitz, J. (2012). Macroeconomic fluctuations, inequality, and economic development. *Journal of Human Development and Capabilities* 13(1), pp. 31–58.

Subramanian, S. V. and Kawachi, I. (2004). Income inequality and health: What have we learned so far? *Epidemiologic Reviews* 26, pp. 78–91.

Takeuschi, L. R. (2014). *When Is Redistribution Popular? Social Conflict and the Politics of Inequality*. ODI Working Paper. http://www.odi.org/sites/odi.org.uk/files/odi-assets/publications-opinion-files/8910.pdf [Accessed 26 Sept. 2015].

UNDP. (2013). *Humanity Divided: Confronting Inequality in Developing Countries*. New York: United Nations Development Program.

UN Human Rights Council. (2015). *Twenty-Ninth Session, Promotion and Protection of All Human Rights, Civil, Political, Economic, Social and Cultural Rights, Including the Right to Development*. A/HRC/29/31. 27 May.

United Nations Declaration on the Right to Development. (1986). A/RES/41/128. Available at: http://www.un.org/documents/ga/res/41/a41r128.htm [Accessed 26 Sept. 2015].

Universal Declaration of Human Rights. (1948). Available at: http://www.ohchr.org/EN/UDHR/Documents/UDHR_Translations/eng.pdf [Accessed 26 Sept. 2015].

Verger, A. and van Paassen, B. (2012). Human development vis-à-vis free trade: understanding developing countries' positions in trade negotiations on education and intellectual property rights. *Review of International Political Economy* 20(4), pp. 712–39.

Wilkinson, R. and Pickett, K. (2009). *The Spirit Level: Why More Equal Societies Almost Always Do Better*. New York: Bloomsbury Press.

World Bank. (2010). *2010 World Development Indicators*. Washington, DC: World Bank. Available at: http://data.worldbank.org/sites/default/files/wdi-final.pdf [Accessed 26 Sept. 2015].

4 A human rights approach to government spending and taxation

Fiscal policy is an essential tool that determines the financial resources governments have at their disposal to implement policies that support the progressive realization of rights. The principle of maximum available resources, based on Article 2.1 of ICESCR (1966), was introduced in Chapter 2. Government spending and taxation are critical for determining the maximum amount of resources available to the state. However, fiscal policy choices often undermine rights, leading to retrogression and unequal outcomes, often through opaque budgetary processes. Fiscal policy is also subject to capture by powerful economic and political groups and institutions, leading to spending and tax policies that benefit specific interests, such as those of global corporations.

This chapter discusses the implications of using a human rights approach to formulate and evaluate fiscal policy—with a primary emphasis on the principle of maximum of available resources.[1] Budgets are critically important tools for realizing rights and there are two sides to any budget—the expenditure side and the revenue side, with taxes being the most significant source of revenues for most governments. The idea of "fiscal space" relates to the budget as a whole, including both expenditure and revenue. It refers to the flexibility, or room, available to a government to adjust elements of its budget in order to increase spending, either overall or in some priority area (UNICEF 2009). A human rights perspective demands that the construction and use of fiscal space be linked to the obligation to use maximum available resources for the realization of human rights and to avoid retrogression. This chapter focuses on the two primary components of fiscal policy: government spending and taxation. Other aspects of the principle of maximum available resources are taken up in the next chapter.

Human rights approaches to fiscal policy

An advantage of expressing the goals of fiscal policy in terms of human rights is that it goes beyond quantitative goals, such as economic growth and full employment, to address other concerns about the role of the economy. Does it produce the goods and services needed to satisfy the right to an adequate standard of living? Does it yield high quality jobs as well as a sufficient quantity of jobs? Moreover, a human rights approach emphasizes that the conduct of fiscal policy should comply with the human rights obligations that governments have entered into. It provides an important arena for deliberation and a normative framework that requires governments to defend their fiscal policy decisions and offers ways of challenging the idea that fiscal policy is a technical matter best left to public finance experts. Government budgets are never the outcomes of a purely technical process based on financial analysis. They are necessarily political documents, as well as instruments of economic policy (Norton and Elson 2002). In the words of Pregs Govender, former chair of the South African Parliamentary Committee on the Improvement of the Quality of Life and Status of Women, "The budget reflects the values of a country—who it values, whose work it values and who it rewards ... and who and what and whose work it doesn't" (quoted in Budlender 1996, p. 7).

The discourse and procedures of human rights positions people as rights holders, especially those who are undervalued, who suffer discrimination, disadvantage, and exclusion. It positions them as active agents, claiming what is rightfully theirs, not as victims asking for charitable hand-outs. It has an ethical authority absent from most economic analysis. The worst that an economist can say of a government's budget is that it is imprudent, unsound, unsustainable, or inefficient, while the human rights advocate can say that it fails to comply with obligations and violates human rights. This may apply even if the budget is deemed to be prudent, sound, sustainable, and efficient by economists.

Government expenditure

There are three central aspects of government expenditures that determine the maximum of available resources for the realization of rights: (1) the overall size of government spending, (2) the allocation of expenditures to specific areas within the budget, and (3) the effective use of those resources to support desired outcomes, such as better education, health, and housing.

To judge how far a government has allocated adequate resources to public expenditure, it is useful to look at the ratio of total expenditure to gross domestic product (GDP). Gross domestic product is a measure of the total value of the output of goods and services produced in the economy, although it leaves out unpaid services in the household, such as unpaid childcare services provided by family members. The expenditure-to-GDP ratio therefore measures a government's public spending relative to the overall size of the market economy. This ratio can be compared between countries as an indicator of whether the governments of countries at similar levels of development have comparable aggregate levels of spending.

Indicators, such as the ratio of public expenditure to GDP, should be thought of as providing broad benchmarks for assessing government policy—they are not meant to be prescriptive targets. There may be valid reasons why government expenditure as a share of GDP will vary from the benchmark. The aim is not to develop precise targets, e.g. 3 percent of GDP must go to education. Instead, the goal is to use such indicators to judge whether there is cause for concern about compliance with obligations of conduct, in comparison with similar countries and with past performance of the same country.[2]

The total amount of expenditure only gives a crude picture of whether governments are mobilizing the maximum of available resources. In addition to looking at the expenditure to GDP ratio, the allocation of spending to particular areas that support the realization of specific rights, e.g. health, education, and income protections and transfers to low-income households, should also be taken into account and compared to areas of spending that do not support human rights, e.g. military spending.

When considering the resources available to realize rights, it is important not to limit the analysis of public expenditures to social spending, since the realization of some economic and social rights, e.g. the right to work, requires an examination of other areas of spending, e.g. public investment in basic economic infrastructure. The scope of human rights expenditure is therefore quite expansive, involving not just social service delivery, but also agricultural, industrial, and employment policy. Consider a case in which efforts to realize children's rights have been exclusively focused on spending on health and education and not on infrastructure investments, such as building roads and schools. Though the spending on health and education can have positive human rights outcomes, the lack of spending on infrastructure may deny some children access to health services and schools—e.g. when the children live far away from the nearest school building or clinic with few or no transportation options. Thus, defining what constitutes a justified investment in economic and social rights should not be limited to social sectors alone, but it should also include investments in economic sectors.

The assessment of fiscal policy using a human rights framework must go beyond an examination of budget allocations. Simply allocating funds to specific uses does not guarantee results on the ground. There is often a gap between budgets and actual delivery. Therefore, as Chapter 2 stressed, there is a need to look at conduct—are the budget allocations sufficient and equitable?—and results—does the budget actually support the fulfillment of rights in terms of realized outcomes? For example, consider the findings of an in-depth analysis of public expenditure and the substantive realization of economic and social rights in Mexico and the US for the period from the early 1980s to the early 2000s (Balakrishnan and Elson

2011). The study crosschecked conduct in terms of fiscal policy with what had been achieved in terms of the enjoyment of rights, mindful that enjoyment of particular rights depends on a wider range of factors than the public expenditure directly linked to that right. The researchers noted that:

implement ation is just as important

> The data on results may reinforce or challenge the conclusions about the conduct of policy. For example, spending public money on health care might be considered to be 'action reasonably calculated to realize' the right to health, but it may not be organized in a way that complies with obligations for non-discrimination and equality. If we find that public expenditure is very unequally distributed between different social groups, this suggests a prime facie case of violation of obligation of conduct. We can cross-check this with data on health status of different social groups (which measure some dimension of how far they enjoy particular levels of the rights to health). If we find the health status of the group with the lowest share of expenditure is worse than those with higher shares of expenditure, this suggests that the government is not in compliance with its obligations of conduct. But if the social group with the lowest share of public expenditure has the highest health status, then this suggests that the needs for public health services of this group are lower, and thus the government may be justified in its conduct of health expenditure.
>
> (Balakrishnan and Elson 2011, p. 15)

It was found that in both Mexico and the US, governments had failed to comply with their obligations in deploying public expenditure in relation to realization of economic and social rights. Take the case of public expenditure on health. As a share of GDP, health expenditure was lower in Mexico in 2006 than in 1980, and per capita health expenditure in Mexico was below that of several comparable large Latin American countries. This does not seem consistent with the principle of using maximum available resources. In addition, the distribution of public expenditure on health did not comply with the obligations for non-discrimination and equality. Public spending per capita on health services for the better-off Mexicans who were covered by contributory social insurance schemes was much higher than the spending on the poorer Mexicans (many of whom are indigenous people) who could only access the much more limited health services supplied by the Ministry of Health.

The health outcomes were disappointing. The child mortality rate had fallen, indicating progressive realization, but remained higher than in many comparable Latin American countries. Brazil had done much better than Mexico in reducing the mortality rates for children under the age of five during the period considered. The national maternal mortality rate appeared to have fallen but remained higher than that of many comparable Latin American countries, and fell far short of government targets for reduction. Moreover, indigenous women were at much greater risk of dying in pregnancy than non-indigenous women, an indicator that health outcomes were not consistent with non-discrimination and equality in the enjoyment of the right to health. An attempt was made to address the acute inequalities in the funding, quality, and accessibility of health services through the introduction of the Popular Insurance scheme in 2003.[3] However, despite increases in the allocation of public expenditure to this new scheme, it continued to exclude much of the rural population and was not effective in prioritizing indigenous communities.

Per capita public expenditure on health care in the US had been rising in real terms: there was no retrogression in terms of the allocation of public expenditure to health care. However, there was no national health insurance program providing universal coverage in the US. Around 15 percent of the population was not covered at all in the period from 1987 to 2009, with racial/ethnic minorities, women, poor people, and migrants all being less likely to have access to health insurance. This calls into question the fulfillment of the obligation to ensure that everyone has access to health care on the basis of non-discrimination and equality.

Many health outcomes were poor: for instance, the US had the fourth highest infant mortality rate in the OECD after Turkey, Mexico and Chile in 2006. Moreover, the rate had risen since 2000, clearly indicating a lack of progressive realization with respect to maternal health. In addition, the maternal mortality rates differed by racial/ethnic group, with the lowest rates for white women and much higher rates for African American women. Once again, these health outcomes were not consistent with non-discrimination and equality in the enjoyment of the right to health. The health care reforms introduced in the US in 2010 did not introduce a comprehensive social insurance system comparable to that of other well-off countries, and there is reason to believe that it will not succeed in ensuring that the right to health is realized in compliance with the obligation for non-discrimination and equality. Comparable deficiencies were found in both Mexico and the US with respect to other programs of public expenditure and other economic and social rights (Balakrishnan and Elson 2011).

Many economists focus on the efficiency of government spending. Efficiency is often defined in terms of the financial costs of the inputs required to produce a particular outcome—greater efficiency implies that more can be produced with a given amount of financial resources. Therefore, from the perspective of utilization of maximum available resources, it is important to examine the efficiency of expenditure.

However, care must be taken when evaluating efficiency. Are all inputs adequately accounted for or are there important resources that are ignored (such as contributions of unpaid household work or other non-market contributions)? For example, in the health sector, efficiency is typically judged in terms of the financial cost per treatment. This can be reduced by shortening the time that patients spend in the hospital. However, patients still need further non-medical care. Therefore, efficiency, narrowly defined, may appear to improve as the cost of providing treatment for each patient drops, but there are substantial spillover costs for unpaid caretakers in households who may be forced to take time off from paid work to care for a family member. Therefore, increasing "efficiency" by reducing spending on key inputs may not create true efficiencies, but it may impose higher costs on unpaid family care at home, with disproportionate impacts on women.

Similarly, efficiency may appear to improve if governments reduce compensation to public sector workers. Under austerity and other budget-cutting policies, states often face pressures to reduce their public-sector wage bill. However, in these cases, we must consider whether such actions compromise the social and economic rights of those workers. If so, then such tactics will be less efficient than they appear to be, since the full impact on social and economic rights must take into account the impact on public sector workers.

It is also important to examine the effectiveness of spending in achieving positive impact on enjoyment of rights. People must be able to claim their rights in ways that do not stigmatize them, something that is especially important in the case of income transfers.

Moreover the quality as well as the quantity of output matters. Services must be delivered in ways that respect the dignity of the recipient, and this requires sufficient time to interact with people and give them personal attention. This is often not possible if there are attempts to increase efficiency by reducing the workforce but maintaining the level of output, as frequently this implies workers having to work faster or perform more than one task at the same time. Public employees must be trained on how to treat people with respect, especially poor people, people from minority groups, and women.

The growing practice of subcontracting the private sector to provide public services further complicates the picture. For example, the subcontracting of health service provision to the private sector in Brazil was integral to a case submitted in 2007 to the Committee on the Elimination of All Forms of Discrimination against Women under the Optional Protocol, which allows the Committee to consider the case of individuals when domestic legal procedures have been exhausted without any remedy being secured. The case was brought by the mother of Alyne da Silva Pimentel Teixeira who had died after childbirth. After considering the evidence submitted on behalf of the complainant and the response of the Brazilian government, in 2011 the CEDAW Committee ruled that Ms. da Silva Pimentel Teixeira did not receive appropriate services in connection with her pregnancy. The Brazilian government argued that the sole responsibility lay with the private sector health care provider contracted to provide health care, but the CEDAW committee ruled that the State is directly responsible for the action of private institutions when it outsources its medical services and that, furthermore, the State always maintains the duty to regulate and monitor private health-care institutions.

(CEDAW 2011, para 7.5)

The ruling applies beyond this case and beyond Brazil in clarifying that the state continues to have human rights responsibilities for the delivery of outsourced services.

The maximum of available resources can be expanded by augmenting public resources with private ones. However, the mobilization of resources from the private sector to meet budgetary objectives raises a number of important questions. One form of leveraging private contributions to public services is through co-responsibility, in which communities are asked to provide unpaid services to support the realization of certain rights, e.g. through the construction of schools. This is not necessarily antithetical to human rights, but we must consider who in the community bears the burden of carrying out these new tasks, and whether such services are voluntarily provided.

A second form of leveraging is through public–private partnerships (PPPs). With PPPs, a government contracts with private companies to carry out infrastructure investment or service provision. In the case of infrastructure investments, the private company raises the money for the investment, not the government, and covers the cost by leasing the assets to the government. This may seem advantageous in the short run, as the borrowing is not included as part of public sector debt. However, in general, private companies face higher rates of interest than governments, so the costs of the investment are higher. In addition, it is difficult to hold the private companies to account for the fulfillment of complex contracts. Typically the contracts transfer risks to the government so that if the enterprise is mismanaged or delivery is poorly implemented, the public sector is forced to assume the burden of correcting the problem. Also the private companies may hire workers with fewer social protections than public sector employees, entailing retrogression with regard to labor rights.[4] Bearing all this in mind, a balanced analysis would consider whether PPPs actually bring in extra resources, explore who is really paying the full set of costs, assess the sustainability of the arrangement over time, and determine what actually is gained with PPPs.

Government spending must also be evaluated in terms of the distribution of benefits among households and individuals. To comply with principles of non-discrimination, public spending should not be allocated in ways which reinforce existing inequalities or which fail to deliver benefits to vulnerable and marginalized populations. The distributive consequences of the allocation of public spending are often referred to as the "incidence" of government expenditures. For example, health budgets that primarily support hospitals and medical facilities that service middle- and upper-income families, and to which low-income populations have limited or no access, will not support the realization of economic and social rights to the same extent as alternative budget allocation.

Human rights activists have been questioning government budgets from a human rights perspective for more than a decade,[5] including in relation to children's rights[6] and women's rights.[7] A few of the many gender budget initiatives[8] that examined budgets from a gender equality perspective had a specific focus on human rights, including the number of gender budget initiatives in the Andean region (Bolivia, Colombia, Ecuador, and Peru). These gender budget initiatives aimed to bring together a wide range of actors from government, legislatures, and civil society within an explicit framework of the promotion of women's economic and social rights (Pearl 2002). The rights-based approach of these initiatives does not take the form of analysis of the quantity of funding allocated to different uses in relation to particular human rights treaties, but rather of analysis of budget processes, especially at the municipal level, to evaluate the extent of women's participation and the scope for enlarging it. They focus in particular on the issues of transparency, participation, and accountability.

There are some examples of city governments seeking to align their budgets and provision of services with their human rights obligations, including San Francisco, Mexico City, and Reykjavik. In 1998 the San Francisco Board of Supervisors and the mayor enacted an ordinance to implement the principles underlying CEDAW even though the US has not ratified CEDAW (Elson 2006, p. 43). The CEDAW ordinance requires the city government to ensure that it will eliminate discrimination and ensure equal opportunity through its budget, employment practices, and provision of services. With the help of the women's rights consulting group Strategic Analysis for Gender Equity (SAGE),[9] a city task force examined the budget and operations of two city departments, the Juvenile Probation Department and the Department of Public Works, in the light of CEDAW. The recommendations focused primarily on better collection of sex-disaggregated data and the creation of a more equal workplace. The analysis that SAGE provided to the city was then revised and implemented within all city departments (SAGE 1999).

In 2009, the city of San Francisco issued a report on the implementation of the CEDAW ordinance. The report provided the following example:

> The city's department of juvenile justice identified the need for a girls advocate on staff, and instituted gender specific programs for young women in the system. The department of public works now takes the safety of women into consideration when choosing the distance between streetlights, and making other night time lighting decisions. They also established a job centre where open positions were posted;

previously an 'old boys' network resulted in many jobs going to friends of current workers.

(Stelzer 2009)

Budget allocations should be determined in ways that are participatory and transparent. The type of participation, at what stage of the budget process it takes place, and the share of the budget open to participation should all be considered. Civil society organizations, including human rights organizations, are now actively engaging with government budgets in many countries. The participation of human rights organizations leads to framing consideration of budgets in terms of government obligations, non-discrimination, progressive realization, core obligations and non-retrogression.

It is important to recognize that strengthening participation and transparency requires resources. Meaningful participation requires the collection and dissemination of timely information—a service that must be paid for. Budget information needs to be compiled in categories that are useful for monitoring spending priorities with regard to social and economic rights, and made accessible to the general population.

A human rights approach to government revenues and taxation

Governments obtain revenue from several sources, including taxation, royalties paid for the utilization of natural resources, and profits from public enterprises. Here we focus on taxation, as this is typically the most important source of revenue. Some economists endorse the idea that taxation is a burden that should be minimized and refer to taxation as something that distorts behavior and creates inefficiency. A human rights perspective shows that taxation is a critical part of complying with the principle of making use of maximum available resources (as explained in Chapter 2). In light of this, it would be more appropriate to refer to tax "contributions" rather than "burdens" and behavioral "incentives/ disincentives" rather than "distortions."

Governments have an obligation of conduct to introduce and implement tax laws and systems of tax administration that are capable of generating sufficient revenue for realization of human rights, in ways that comply with other human rights obligations, such as non-discrimination and equality, transparency, accountability and participation. For example, in the study of Mexico and the US mentioned earlier, taxation and human rights obligations were empirically analyzed for the period of the late 1980s to the mid-2000s (Balakrishnan and Elson 2011). It was found that neither the government of Mexico nor the US had been conducting tax policy in ways that fully comply with human rights obligations.

Tax revenue in Mexico as a share of GDP was low compared to other Latin American countries and tax administration was poor, permitting significant tax evasion and avoidance. This suggests a lack of compliance with the obligation to use maximum available resources. Though in Mexico, a high proportion of government revenue comes from revenues and royalties from PEMEX, the state-owned oil company, recently there has been a move to privatize PEMEX. In addition, since oil is a non-renewable natural resource, and prices are volatile, it is not a reliable source of revenue.

With regard to non-discrimination and equality, personal income tax in Mexico was progressive, with the higher income groups paying a larger share of their income in income tax than the lower income groups. There was no explicit discrimination against women, as income tax is levied on individuals even if they are married, but the relative inability of women earners to take advantage of tax allowances was a problem because the allowances were only available for employees—not for the self-employed— and women are more likely to be self-employed. Value added tax (VAT), levied on most goods and services, and therefore paid by all Mexicans, was regressive in terms of its incidence on household income. The incidence of VAT in conjunction with other indirect taxes on drinks, tobacco, and fuel, was found to be higher on households with children in which women contributed 60 percent or more of the earnings, as compared to other households, again suggesting indirect discrimination against women.

The Federal Law of Transparency and Access to Public Information introduced in Mexico in 2003 had led to some improvement in accountability and participation, including in mechanisms to hold those who break the tax law to account, but tax evasion and avoidance remain high.

In the US, tax revenue as a share of GDP was lower than in comparable rich countries, calling into question whether the government has been mobilizing the maximum of available resources. Over time, the share of revenue coming from corporations had fallen and that coming from individuals had risen. Tax on the incomes of the very wealthy had fallen, compromising the principles of equality and non-discrimination. In relation to gender equality, the system of personal income tax income created a disincentive for married women to participate in the labor market because the tax is levied on married couples through a joint-filing system, on their joint income. Insofar as married women tend to be the secondary earners in the household, this means that they face a higher effective tax rate on the first dollar they earn than they would face as an individual, because their earnings are added to those of their husband.

Sales and local taxes levied by state and local governments were regressive with respect to household income, and since African-Americans and Latinos were more likely to have lower incomes than white Americans, they were likely to be harder hit by these taxes.

Although the tax authorities were charged with providing information about the tax code to the public, the code is complex and opaque so that those who cannot afford the advice of specialist tax accountants find it hard to understand; and those who can afford this advice, especially corporations, find many loopholes for tax avoidance. The tax system was found to be tilted in favor of corporations and the wealthy, and the principle of non-discrimination and equality was breached in several ways in the tax system. To rectify this, and to allow the state to use maximum available resources, Balakrishnan and Elson (2011) concluded that the tax system needs to be reformed to ensure more revenue is raised in ways that comply with human rights obligations.

Raising the amount of revenue collected may require a combination of increasing tax rates, introducing new taxes, and improving tax collection. In a number of sub-Saharan African countries, the efficiency of revenue collection has been enhanced through institutional reforms in the way that taxes are administered and collected, independent of changes in tax policy (OECD and ADB 2010). Tax avoidance and evasion lead to substantial loss of revenue for governments. Bribery and corruption of tax officials are also common problems in many countries. It is vital to strengthen tax collection processes to support progressive realization of rights. Cutting the budgets of tax collection offices is a false economy, as it means that fewer people are available to curtail avoidance and evasion.

The existence of tax havens—most of which are located in, or under the jurisdiction of, wealthy countries—facilitates tax avoidance and evasion. More than $21 trillion in private assets are reported to be held in tax havens to evade and avoid taxes (Henry 2012). Multinational corporations take advantage of tax havens to reduce tax payments. By setting up headquarters in a tax haven geography, then manipulating the price of imports purchased from and exports shipped to other divisions and affiliates of the same company operating in different countries, corporations can show their profits as accruing in a tax haven rather than in a country with higher taxes. Estimates of the annual tax revenue lost to developing countries due to this kind of tax avoidance and evasion amount to 98–106 billion USD (Hollingshead 2010). This compares to total overseas development assistance in 2009 from OECD countries of 83.5 billion USD (Elson, Balakrishnan and Heintz 2013, p. 28). Cooperation among states is vital to reduce the scope for cross-border tax avoidance strategies.

Individual countries, in particular low-income countries, are severely constrained in the measures that they alone can take against tax abuse. The availability of offshore financial centers (tax havens) that offer low or no taxes and secrecy is a major factor. As noted by Sepúlveda (2014), governments that facilitate or actively promote tax abuse and other illicit financial flows through their tax secrecy laws are jeopardizing their compliance with their human rights obligations. Therefore, they should take coordinated measures against tax evasion globally as part of both domestic and extraterritorial human rights obligations and to fulfill their duty to protect people from human rights violations by third parties, including business enterprises. There are some international treaties on cross-border financial flows, but they are totally inadequate to deal with a globalized economy. The OECD has been coordinating action to try to deal with this (OECD 2013) but progress is slow.

There is potential for the introduction of new taxes, such as financial transaction taxes (FTT). This is a levy on a particular type of transaction in the financial sector. A report from an independent Washington, DC-based think tank, the Tax Policy Center (Burman et al. 2015) points out that many countries already have some form of financial transaction tax and that 11 European Union (EU) countries have agreed to enact a coordinated FTT that is scheduled to go into effect in January 2016. Estimates for the US indicate that a financial transaction tax set at 50 basis points for equities (i.e. stocks), 15 basis points for bonds, and 0.5 basis points for derivatives could generate approximately $350 billion in revenue, taking into account potential reductions in trading volume (Pollin and Heintz 2012). A basis point is one-hundredth of a percent, so a 50 basis point tax would be a tax of 0.5 percent of the value of the stock being traded. Schulmeister et al. (2009) have estimated the amount that could be raised globally from an FTT applied to all non-retail markets, including foreign exchange, exchange-traded, and OTC derivatives. They found that a tax at 0.1 percent would generate revenues of $917 billion, while a 0.05 percent rate would generate $650 billion.

One objection raised by some economists is that higher taxes on businesses and wealthy households will reduce investment and, hence, growth and employment. Such an impact could conceivably limit the generation of resources available for realizing economic and social rights—thereby affecting the maximum resources available. Engen and Skinner (1996), using a standard growth model, provide a summary of why taxes might affect economic growth. However, they present empirical findings that show only a modest impact of taxes on growth. This may be because lower tax rates and various kinds of tax allowances may just be windfall gains for businesses and wealthy households who would have invested anyway. The primary reasons companies invest (e.g. market access, the availability of an educated labor force, strategic export platforms, or the presence of natural resources) tend to have little to do with tax levels. Recent empirical research at the IMF found that redistribution through taxation and transfers "appears generally benign in terms of its impact on growth; only in extreme cases is there some evidence that it may have direct negative effects on growth" (Ostry, Berg, and Tsangarides 2014, p. 4). They conclude that "the average redistribution, and the associated reduction in inequality, is thus associated with higher and more durable growth" (Ibid., p. 28).

Looking at taxation through a human rights lens helps to build the case for reforms that boost government revenues, especially from the better-off and from corporations, and provides an umbrella under which a variety of civil society groups can push for changes in tax policy. Saiz (2013) documents how activists in Guatemala were able to use a report on taxation and the rights to health, education, and food to secure a commitment in 2009 from the Minister of Finance to introduce progressive tax reforms. Counter-pressure from business interests prevented the minister from doing this. A human rights approach is thus not a panacea, but framing tax reform in terms of human rights provides a new energizing discourse in which struggles for tax justice can take place. These synergies were recognized in the Lima Declaration (2015) that was endorsed by a "broad-based community of experienced advocates, practitioners, activists, scholars, jurists, litigators and others committed to advancing tax justice through human rights and to realizing human rights through just tax policy."[10] Advocacy of higher taxes on businesses and well-off people is often dismissed as the politics of envy. We can recast this advocacy as the politics of human rights and point to the obligations that governments have to raise revenue for realizing human rights.

✱ A₿ C

Conclusion

This chapter presented an approach to fiscal policy that takes into account human rights principles and obligations, with a specific focus on the principle of maximum of available resources. This approach helps to shift the terms of the debate about fiscal policy from a concern with a narrowly defined understanding of efficiency towards one that is focused on realized outcomes for social justice. It provides tools for assessing a government's compliance with the human rights approach and for evaluating the expenditure and taxation policies governments adopt. This provides a means of exploring alternatives to the dominant approach to fiscal policy and assessing whether, as required by the obligation of conduct, a given set of fiscal policies are "reasonably calculated" to realize the enjoyment of economic and social rights.

Notes

1   This chapter draws on the conceptual arguments in Elson, Balakrishnan, and Heintz (2013) and Balakrishnan et al. (2011).
2   The empirical examples draw on Balakrishnan and Elson (2011).
3   In 2003 the General Health Bill was reformed and a new program, Popular Insurance (Seguro Popular), with limited health protection for the uninsured population, was created.
4   For an overview of public–private partnerships, see Hodge, Greve, and Boardman 2010; for a discussion of these issues in relation to the UK see the *Guardian* (2001) and Vize (2015).
5   See for example Schultz (2002).
6   See for example Streak and Wehner (2002).
7   See for example Hofbauer (2000).
8   There is a large literature on gender budget initiatives, or gender responsive budgeting, covering analytical tools, training handbooks, analysis by civil society groups and academics, and government reports. For a recent overview see Quinn (2013). NGO reports and reports by UN agencies and governments

may be found on a website run by UN Women: http://genderfinancing.
unwomen.org/en/resources.
9 Radhika Balakrishnan was a member of SAGE.
10 Radhika Balakrishnan was among the group that originated the Lima
   Declaration.

References

Balakrishnan, R. and Elson, D. (2011). Introduction. In: R. Balakrishnan and
    D. Elson, eds., *Economic Policy and Human Rights: Holding Governments to
    Account*. London: Zed Books, pp. 1–27.
Balakrishnan, R., Elson, D., Heintz, J., and Lusiani, N. (2011). *Maximum Available
    Resources & Human Rights: Analytical Report*. New Brunswick, NJ: Center for
    Women's Global Leadership, Rutgers University.
Budlender, D., ed. (1996). *The Women's Budget*. Cape Town: Institute for Democracy
    in South Africa.
Burman, L., Gale, W., Gault, S., Kim, B., Nunns, J., and Rosenthal, S. (2015).
    Financial Transactions Taxes in Theory and Practice. Washington, DC: Tax Policy
    Center, Urban Institute and Brookings Institution.
Committee on the Elimination of All Forms of Discrimination against Women
    (CEDAW). (2011). *Views of the Committee on the Elimination of Discrimination
    against Women under Article 7, Paragraph 3, of the Optional Protocol to the Convention
    on the Elimination of All Forms of Discrimination against Women*, Communication
    No. 17/2008, CEDAW/C/49/D/17/2008.
Elson, D. (2006). *Budgeting for Women's Rights: Monitoring Government Budgets for
    Compliance with CEDAW*. New York: UNIFEM. Available at: http://es.unrol.
    org/doc.aspx?n=MonitoringGovernmentBudgetsComplianceCEDAW_eng.
    pdf [Accessed 15 Sept. 2015].
Elson, D., Balakrishnan, R., and Heintz, J. (2013). Public finance, maximum
    available resources and human rights. In: A. Nolan, R. O'Connell, and
    C. Harvey, eds., *Human Rights and Public Finance: Budget Analysis and the
    Advancement of Economic and Social Rights*. Oxford: Hart Publishing, pp. 13–40.
Engen, E. and Skinner, J. (1996). Taxation and economic growth. *National Tax
    Journal*, 49(4), pp. 617–42.
Guardian. (2001). Public–Private Partnerships. Available at: http://www.
    theguardian.com/society/ppp/0,10537,509342,00.html [Accessed 15 Sept.
    2015].
Henry, J. (2012). The price of offshore revisited. *Tax Justice Network*, July. Available
    at: http://www.taxjustice.net/cms/upload/pdf/The_Price_of_Offshore_
    Revisited_Presser_120722.pdf [Accessed 15 Sept. 2015].
Hodge, G., Greve, C., and Boardman, A. E., eds. (2010). *International Handbook on
    Public–Private Partnerships*. Cheltenham: Edward Elgar Publishing.
Hofbauer, H. (2000). *Women, Human Rights and Budget Analysis*. Cuernavaca:
    FUNDAR, and Cape Town: Women's Economic Equality Project.
Hollingshead, A. (2010). *The Implied Tax Revenue Loss from Trade Mispricing*.
    Washington, DC: Global Financial Integrity. Available at: http://www.
    gfintegrity.org/storage/gfip/documents/reports/implied%20tax%20
    revenue%20loss%20report_final.pdf [Accessed 15 Sept. 2015].

International Covenant on Economic, Social and Cultural Rights (ICESCR). (1966). Office of the High Commissioner for Human Rights. Available at: http://www.ohchr.org/EN/ProfessionalInterest/Pages/CESCR.aspx [Accessed 26 Sept. 2015].

Lima Declaration on Tax Justice and Human Rights. (2015) Available at: http://www.cesr.org/downloads/Lima_Declaration_Tax_Justice_Human_Rights.pdf [Accessed 15 Sept. 2015].

Norton, A. and Elson, D. (2002). *What's Behind the Budget? Politics, Rights and Accountability in the Budget Process*. London: Overseas Development Institute.

OECD. (2013). *Action Plan on Base Erosion and Profit Shifting*. Paris: Organisation for Economic Cooperation and Development.

OECD and ADB. (2010). *African Economic Outlook 2010*. Paris: Organisation for Economic Cooperation and Development and African Development Bank.

Ostry, J., Berg, A., and Tsangarides, C. (2014). *Redistribution, Inequality and Growth*. IMF Staff Discussion Note, February. Washington, DC: IMF.

Pearl, R. (2002). The Andean Region: A multi-country program. In: D. Budlender and G. Hewitt, eds., *Gender Budgets Make More Cents. Country Studies and Good Practice*. London: Commonwealth Secretariat, pp. 23–42.

Pollin, R. and Heintz, J. (2012). *Thoughts on Tax Rates and Revenue Potential for Financial Transaction Tax in U.S. Financial Markets. Memo to Robin Hood Tax Coalition*. Amherst, MA: Political Economy Research Institute. Available at: http://www.peri.umass.edu/fileadmin/pdf/ftt/Pollin--Heintz--Memo_on_FTT_Rates_and_Revenue_Potential_w_references----6-9-12.pdf [Accessed 15 Sept. 2015].

Quinn, S. (2013) Equality proofing the budget: Lessons from the experience of gender budgeting. In: Nolan, A., O'Connell, R., and Harvey, C., eds., *Human Rights and Public Finance: Budget Analysis and the Advancement of Economic and Social Rights*. Oxford: Hart Publishing.

SAGE (Strategic Analysis for Gender Equality & San Francisco Commission on the Status of Women). (1999). *Guidelines for a Gender Analysis of City Departments in the City and County of San Francisco*. San Francisco: Commission on Status of Women.

Streak, J. and Wehner, J. (2002). *Budgeting for Socio-Economic Rights in South Africa: The Case of the Child Support Grant Program*. Cape Town: Institute for Democracy in South Africa.

Saiz, I. (2013). Resourcing rights: Combating tax injustice from a human rights perspective. In: A. Nolan, R. O'Connell and C. Harvey, eds., *Human Rights and Public Finance: Budget Analysis and the Advancement of Economic and Social Rights*. Oxford: Hart Publishing, pp. 77–106.

Schulmeister, S., Schratzenstaller, M., and Picek, O. (2009). *A General Financial Transaction Tax: A Short Cut of the Pros, the Cons and a Proposal*. Vienna: Österreichisches Institut für Wirtschaftsforschung (WIFO), September.

Sepúlveda, M. C. (2014). *Report of the Special Rapporteur on Extreme Poverty and Human Rights*. A/HRC/26/28. Available at: http://www.ohchr.org/EN/Issues/Poverty/Pages/AnnualReports.aspx [Accessed 15 Sept. 2015].

Shultz, J. (2002). *Promises to Keep: Using Public Budgets as a Tool to Advance Economic, Social and Cultural Rights*. Conference Report. Mexico City: Ford Foundation and FUNDAR.

Stelzer, A. (2009). Gender: For U.S., lessons in CEDAW from San Francisco. *Inter Press Service News Agency*. Available at: http://www.ipsnews.net/2009/11/gender-for-us-lessons-in-cedaw-from-san-francisco/ [Accessed 24 Sept. 2015].

UNICEF. (2009). *Fiscal Space and Public Expenditure on the Social Sectors*. February Briefing Paper, February 2009. Available at: www.unicef.org/wcaro/wcaro_08_UNICEF_OPM_briefing_paper__Fiscal_Space.pdf [Accessed 15 Sept. 2015].

Vize, R. (2015) PFI is an unaffordable mistake for the NHS. *Guardian*. Available at: http://www.theguardian.com/healthcare-network/2015/aug/28/corbyn-right-pfi-unaffordable-mistake-nhs [Accessed 15 Sept. 2015].

5 Mobilizing resources to realize rights

Debt, aid, and monetary policy

The International Covenant on Economic, Social and Cultural Rights states that a government must take steps "to the maximum of its available resources" to support the progressive realization of human rights (ICESCR 1966). But what does the principle of maximum available resources actually mean? Many policy-makers and academics adopt a conservative approach, taking the available resources as already having been set by policy choices. The government's job is then to choose the best way to use those fixed resources to realize rights. In practice, this means focusing on the national budget, taking the parameters of that budget as given. However, the amount of resources available to government is also determined by deliberate policy decisions. For example, as Chapter 4 shows, tax policy will directly influence public revenues and the resources at the government's disposal. This chapter takes the principle of maximum available resources further and looks at how deficit financing, official development assistance, and central bank policy can push the envelope even more.

This is not to argue that the resources available to governments are unlimited or costless. Debt burdens can become unsustainable and limit, rather than enhance, policy choices. Overreliance on international assistance can lead to unwanted dependencies. Irresponsible monetary policy can contribute to excessively high rates of inflation or capital outflows. However, the policy space available to expand the resources available to increase the enjoyment of rights is greater than conventional economic policy would lead us to believe. The human rights framework demands that we take these options seriously when designing the policies that would support the fullest realization of basic human rights.

This chapter focuses on the principle of maximum available resources in the areas of debt, international assistance, and monetary policy. However, it is important to bear in mind that other human rights principles and obligations are relevant. These include non-discrimination and equality, accountability, transparency, and participation. Do monetary policies reduce or exacerbate gender inequalities? How are decisions made with respect to the level of debt, the use of official development assistance, and central bank priorities? Do international institutions support or undermine a government's ability to take actions to support the realization of rights? These, and similar questions, are relevant to a human rights approach to these macroeconomic policy issues.[1]

Debt and deficit financing

Chapter 4 discussed the principle of maximum available resources within the context of fiscal policy, government spending and taxation. However, total government spending is not limited to the revenues available in a particular year. When government spending exceeds total government revenue there is a budget deficit and governments must borrow to make up the difference. Governments borrow by taking loans from other governments, commercial banks, and international financial institutions like the IMF and World Bank. Governments also borrow by issuing bonds to investors.

Bonds stipulate the conditions under which the government must pay back the money it borrows. That is, the bond specifies the size of the payments to the bondholders and the length of time over which the bond must be repaid. These conditions of repayment are fixed for each bond. Short-term bonds are paid back quickly, often within a few months, while long-term bonds are repaid over a much longer period, often many years. Bonds are bought and sold in the bond market, and once the government issues a bond, it can be traded among investors in global markets. The price of the bonds varies with conditions in the bond market. If a government has difficulty finding investors willing to hold its bonds, the price of the bonds falls until they are sold. From the government's point of view, lower bond prices means that borrowing has become more expensive, since the sale of bonds generates fewer resources. From the investors' point of view, lower prices mean a higher rate of return, since the investor has to pay less money initially in exchange for the future payments the government must make as stipulated by the bond.

It is important to recognize the difference between budget deficits and the public debt. Deficits represent how much is borrowed to cover the gap between revenues and expenditures in a particular budget. The total amount that a government borrows over time, i.e. the total outstanding amount owed to bondholders and other creditors, is the public debt. The public debt represents a claim on future budgets as interest has to be paid.

In some cases, formal limitations exist that constrain the ability of governments to borrow. These restrictions may come from laws or constitutional restrictions and may only apply to a particular level of government, e.g. state, provincial, or local governments. Or the limitations may exist because donors and lenders, such as the International Monetary Fund, place restrictions on the government's ability to borrow as a condition associated with their financial support.

Since borrowing expands the resources available to government to finance the realization of human rights, it raises the threshold on the maximum level of resources the government has at its disposal in the current time period. However, public debt implies that, in the future, creditors have a claim on future government revenues, which can constrain fiscal space in subsequent periods. So when is borrowing to support the fulfillment of rights a good idea?

To answer this question we need to look at the two sides of the balance sheet, liabilities on one side (i.e. borrowing) and assets on the other. In deciding whether borrowing can contribute to or hinder the realization of human rights, it is critical to consider whether the government is using the debt to finance investments that will help in the realization of economic and social rights. Conventional arguments on debt burdens frequently fail to address the asset side. In other words, if a government borrows, what assets will it be able to create that would not have been created otherwise? For instance, improving transportation infrastructure raises future productivity. Building a new school represents an investment in the future.

In defining assets that contribute to realization of human rights, investments in human beings must be included, as well as investments in physical capital (UN Women 2015). There is no point in building a school if teachers are not also provided. These kinds of investments can also raise the productivity of private investments; they complement, rather than compete with private investment. Enhanced productivity supports faster growth and higher incomes that, in turn, increase tax revenues and allow governments to pay back the initial borrowing over time. Public investments in education, health, and infrastructure also attract more private investment and may be decisive in investment decisions. These investments support long-run growth and generate the resources needed to meet future debt obligations, as well as supporting the realization of human rights.[2]

Two key questions arise when considering whether borrowing might positively or negatively affect human rights. First, to what extent are assets financed through borrowing contributing to human rights? If the assets are not improving human rights processes or outcomes, obviously the need for such borrowing should be questioned. Second, will those assets generate income through economic activities that directly or indirectly repay the debt, or at least the interest payments? Investments in nutrition and education, for example, make some people more productive, which will increase output. Provided there is a way of taxing this output, the debt can be serviced by higher tax revenue.

A further consideration is the overall state of the economy. Borrowing in a recession and borrowing in good times are very different. During a downturn, government spending represents an important policy instrument to stimulate economic activity and get the economy going again. Deficit financing plays a central role in allowing governments to increase expenditures in recessions, because government revenues fall during recessions. Without the ability to borrow, governments may have to cut spending in response to declining revenues, making the downturn worse. During periods of stable growth, these deficits can be repaid when government revenues recover. The use of deficit financing to support government spending during downturns, and then paying back this borrowing when growth has recovered, is referred to as "counter-cyclical fiscal policy."

Debt servicing payments also depend on macroeconomic variables, such as the prevailing interest rates and exchange rates. Monetary policy influences interest rates and exchange rates, an issue discussed later in this chapter. In addition, the types of bonds that governments issue and the nature of the bond market have a direct influence on the costs of borrowing. Some governments rely primarily on short-term bonds. In these cases, governments must continually issue new bonds when existing bonds come due, and debt management is more burdensome and uncertain. When new bonds are issued, they may not generate the same resources as the older bonds because of changing conditions in the bond market. In addition, the composition of buyers and sellers in bond markets affects the cost of servicing the debt. For example, in many sub-Saharan African countries, the domestic banking sector purchases the vast majority of bonds (Heintz 2013). This gives the banks a great deal of power to influence the price at which governments can sell their bonds.

Public borrowing may also have consequences for the distribution of income. Interest payments on the debt go to those who own the bonds or issue loans. The ownership of public debt is often highly concentrated, therefore, debt servicing payments may represent a transfer of income to wealthier segments of the global economy. Committing to large debt payments involves future transfers from the government to wealth holders. If the government has to tax low-income and middle-class households to pay this interest, then there is redistribution from the poor to the rich. These regressive impacts need to be brought into the analysis and might suggest the need for alternative policies, such as the progressive taxation examples discussed in Chapter 4.

Recognizing the impact high levels of indebtedness can have on the fulfillment of rights, in 2000, the Commission on Human Rights, which was replaced by the Human Rights Council, decided to appoint an independent expert on the effects of foreign debt on the full enjoyment of human rights. In 2004, the independent expert was asked to develop guidelines to ensure that debt repayments do not undermine economic and social rights obligations. These guidelines fed into a process to create the Guiding Principles on Foreign Debt and Human Rights, which, in 2012, was submitted to and endorsed by the Human Rights Council.

The Guiding Principles on Foreign Debt and Human Rights states that all States should pursue effective policies and measures aimed at creating the conditions for ensuring the full realization of all human rights, bearing in mind the indivisibility, interdependence and interrelatedness of all human rights and taking into account the potentially negative impact on the enjoyment of human rights of external debt servicing and the adoption of related economic reform policies.

(Lumina 2011, principle 7)

At the same time, it is important to keep in mind the positive role that debt can play in realizing rights, as discussed previously. In a 2011 report to the Human Rights Council, the Independent Expert on Foreign Debt and Human Rights stated "depending on a variety of factors, such as responsible lending and borrowing, the loan terms and conditions, prudent use of loans and proper debt management, debt financing can contribute to countries' economic development and the establishment of conditions for the realization of human rights" (Lumina 2011, para 3).

The concepts of onerous, odious, and illegitimate debt provide tools with which to analyze the implications of accumulated debt.[3] Onerous debt generally refers to a situation in which the obligations attached to the debt, for example debt-servicing, payments significantly exceed the benefits that were derived from taking on the debt. In these circumstances, the cost of servicing the debt can greatly limit the ability of the state to progressively realize rights. Odious and illegitimate debt refer to situations in which the national debt was incurred by a regime for purposes that do not serve the interests of the nation, e.g. the debt enriched economic elites or was used to finance war or repression.[4] Again, sizeable debts that did not advance human rights compromise the ability of the state to make progress towards realizing those rights in the future.

The sustainability of debt also very much depends on the creditors. Views and expectations of creditors can be volatile, especially in times of economic crisis. Austerity measures that some governments have undertaken are an attempt to restore the confidence of bondholders in order to convince them to continue to hold the bonds. Nevertheless, bondholders have been demanding higher rates of return in exchange for agreeing to hold the debt of some governments. This raises the payments governments must make to service the debt. In the context of an economic downturn, when government revenues are already under pressure, higher debt-serving payments squeeze other areas of spending. There is a danger that obligations to creditors can overwhelm the obligation to protect and progressively realize human rights.

In addition, creditors may demand policy changes as a condition of extending additional borrowing, as typified by the structural adjustment programs of the World Bank and the International Monetary Fund in the 1980s and the 1990s. Policy conditionalities tied to borrowing are discussed in greater detail in Chapters 6 and 8. Here we simply recognize that some of the policies required, such as tax cuts that limit government spending, have implications for the principle of maximum of available resources. These dynamics are recognized in the Guiding Principles on Foreign Debt and Human Rights:

> International financial organizations and private corporations have an obligation to respect international human rights. This implies a duty to refrain from formulating, adopting, funding and implementing policies and programmes which directly or indirectly contravene the enjoyment of human rights.
>
> (2012; Principle 9)

The sovereign debt crisis in the European Union, a direct result of the 2008 global financial crisis, illustrates these dynamics. The debt crisis resulted from the inability of smaller Eurozone countries to finance their public debt, specifically Greece, Ireland, and Portugal. Rising debt-servicing costs created a situation in which public debt in the European crisis countries was no longer sustainable (Blundell-Wignall and Slovik 2011). Rescue packages were organized to stabilize the situation.[5] The rescue packages included emergency loans and agreements to restructure the debts to make the debt-servicing payments affordable. However, the rescue packages also included conditionalities requiring large cuts to government spending. The cost of adjusting to the financial crisis therefore reduced the ability of these governments to mobilize the maximum resources to realize human rights. These issues are taken up in depth in Chapter 8.

Official development assistance

Article 2.1 of the ICESCR emphasizes that the principle of maximum available resources also involves "international assistance and cooperation, especially economic and technical" (ICESCR 1966). Article 4.1 of the Declaration on the Right to Development (1986) also states that "states have the duty to take steps, individually and collectively, to formulate international development policies with a view to facilitating the full realization of the rights to development." Both documents recognize the importance of international cooperation in providing resources to governments to fulfill economic, social, and cultural rights.

Official Development Assistance (ODA) can augment the resources available to governments, particularly developing countries with low levels of domestic resource mobilization. It is provided both bilaterally, government to government, and by multilateral institutions such as the World Bank, regional development banks, and regional bodies, such as the European Union. ODA may finance specific projects, such as the building of a hospital or a bridge, but increasing amounts of ODA are not tied to a specific project. They are provided to augment the budget of specific ministries ("sector support") or to the Ministry of Finance to support the budget as a whole ("budget support"). ODA that is not tied to a project generally has policy conditions attached to it, such as trade liberalization, an increasing role for the private sector in service provision, or ceilings on public sector pay. Not all ODA provides extra resources for the government; some ODA bypasses the government and goes directly to non-government organizations. A useful indicator for how far governments extend international assistance is the value of ODA as a proportion of GDP. A widely used benchmark is that high income countries should provide ODA amounting to 0.7 percent of GNI (gross national income).[6]

Though this can be an important source of revenue for governments there are some potential problems as well. ODA does not always come in the form of grants. Instead, assistance is given as loans that need to be paid back with interest. These payments, the debt service and the amortization of loans, mean that not all of the ODA that flows into a country any one year is a net addition to the resources available to the government. The net inflows rather than gross inflow provide a better picture of the resources actually available to a government and even then debt relief is often counted as part of net ODA.

There are also several reasons that make ODA problematic in terms of government's sustained ability to fulfill the obligation to provide the maximum of available resources. If governments are very dependent on ODA as a proportion of government revenue they are vulnerable to the variability in aid flows. If ODA is pro-cyclical, meaning it contracts when there is a downturn in the donor country's economy, this can exacerbate the impact of a downturn in the receiving country. ODA can also be volatile and unpredictable, making it hard to plan expenditures. A great deal of aid does not reach the country and often is given to intermediaries, so though the amount of money seems to increase, the actual impact in terms of government budgets might be small (UNDP 2011).

The impact of ODA on available resources will be reduced if ODA is tied to the purchases of imports from donor countries that cost more than goods and services available locally or on the international market. The proportion of bilateral aid that is formally untied rose from 46 percent in 1999–2000 to 76 percent in 2007; however, research has found that in most investment projects, the main contract and technical assistance are still procured from donor countries, so some of the ODA that has flowed into a recipient country almost immediately flows back out again to the donor (Clay, Geddes, and Natali 2009).

It is sometimes argued that recipient countries may not be able to absorb additional amounts of ODA because they lack the capacity to spend it effectively. However, if this is the case, ODA could be directed towards increasing this capacity. A further argument is that if countries spend their additional ODA, it will lead to inflation rather than mobilization of real resources. The IMF, for instance, argued in 2007 that low-income countries should keep much of their additional ODA in their foreign exchange reserves rather than spend it, unless they have very low rates of inflation (IMF 2007).

Another concern is that ODA may substitute for tax revenues rather than augmenting available resources. Large amounts of aid could serve as a disincentive for governments to increase the effectiveness of their tax collection systems. However, the policy conditions attached to aid may themselves make tax collection more difficult. For example, trade liberalization is often a policy requirement, but this requires a reduction of taxes on import.

The effective use of ODA to support human rights depends not only on recipient governments, but also on donor governments. Much ODA is distributed more in accordance with the political interests of donor countries than the needs of recipient countries. Moreover, donor governments and institutions attach policy conditions to ODA in the belief that this will lead to more effective use of ODA, but these have often been counterproductive.

There is a need to rethink international cooperation in ways that go beyond a narrow focus on development assistance and making aid work for developing countries.[7] A new approach to international cooperation should be grounded in the various human rights treaties and agreements, including the Declaration on the Right to Development. This entails an internationally coordinated approach to development policies and programs, the involvement of UN treaty bodies and specialized agencies to promote a human rights-based approach to development, as well as mechanisms that hold international financial institutions and other donor bodies accountable to international human rights principles and obligations.

The future vision for how development should be financed was discussed at the Financing for Development (FFD) meeting that took place in July 2015 in Addis Ababa, Ethiopia. This meeting was supposed to determine how the future global development agenda—referred to as the post-2015 development agenda—would be financed. It included deliberations on the role of ODA.[8] The outcome document from the meeting, called the Addis Ababa Action Agenda, reflected a much more pronounced role for the private sector and domestic resource mobilization. There is mention in the document of the importance of social protection, and it acknowledges the need to have developed countries meet their ODA obligations, as they have fallen short of these goals (Maxwell 2015). There were actually no new ODA commitments made in FFD, just a reaffirmation of existing 0.7 percent of GNI commitment and some focus on least developed countries (LDCs). The European Union, the United States, Australia, and Japan placed the onus of financing development on domestic resource mobilization, a departure from the historic obligation of developed countries to contribute to development (Regions Refocus et al. 2015).

Even though there was a great deal of emphasis on domestic resource mobilization, there was no agreement on the creation of an international tax body that could regulate tax avoidance and tax evasion, and democratize global economic governance in tax policy in all countries, including least developed countries, who are the most adversely affected by the lack of global tax cooperation. As Bhumika Muchhala (2015) stated: "The hallmark failure of the 3rd FFD [Financing for Development] conference is the missed opportunity to create an intergovernmental tax body, despite the persistent push into the 11th hour by a critical mass of developed countries led by India and Brazil. Such a global tax body, that would enable the UN to have a norm-setting role in tax cooperation at an equal capacity to that of the current monopoly role of the OECD, would have been a meaningful advancement in global economic governance and domestic resource mobilisation in least developed countries.".

Another shift that took place at the Addis Ababa meeting and in the post-2015 development agenda process is the emphasis on the role of the private sector as a critical source of money for development as well as the implementation of the broader development agenda. This emphasis on the private sector began much earlier and has been a recurring theme across global, regional, and national bodies, including development banks, the International Financial Institutions (IFIs) and the UN. The World Bank in its report on financing for development for post-2015 states

> Achieving development goals will require the mobilization of resources from private sources, including FDI [foreign direct investment], bank loans, capital markets, and private transfers (e.g., remittances). For most developing countries, FDI is the preferred private financing modality given its potential to strengthen productivity and growth, and help diversify the economy.
>
> (World Bank Group 2013)

One of the critical and disturbing aspects of the post-2015 development agenda is the diversion of responsibility for development away from the state and to the private sector, public–private partnerships, and other financial instruments (Adams and Martens 2015). It is disturbing because the private sector does not recognize the developmental role of the state and the need for the state to fulfill its obligations to respect, protect, and fulfill rights. No real mechanisms have been put in place to ensure that resources being used from the private sector are being used for the achievement of economic, social, and cultural rights—raising questions of whether the maximum available resources will be used to realize rights over time (Muchhala 2015). This is a clear step away from the obligation to international cooperation made in the Declaration on the Right to Development and the ICESCR.

Monetary and financial policies

Central banks issue currency, influence the amount of credit in the economy, regulate private banks and other financial institutions, and influence critical prices in the economy, such as interest rates and exchange rates. Central banks also operate as "lenders of last resort," providing credit when the financial sector is in crisis. Although central banks are generally statutory institutions—created by the state and operating under government mandates—most central banks enjoy a high degree of independence from other areas of government policy-making. Despite this independence, central banks *are* public institutions, and it can be argued that they also have human rights obligations. These include the obligation to protect rights from the actions of private financial institutions and to channel financial resources to support the realization of rights.

Central banks formulate and implement monetary policy, which directly affects the resources available for the realization of rights. Monetary policy also influences the cost of those resources through its impact on interest rates and exchange rates. Higher interest rates discourage borrowing and make credit more expensive—as a consequence, economic activity slows. This may contribute to unemployment as firms cut back on hiring. Slower growth can also reduce tax revenues that governments rely on for social and economic policies. Higher interest rates affect the sustainability of debt—both public and private—and may cause governments to cut expenditures when interest payments on the public debt rise. If the principle of "maximum available resources" applies to financial resources, then the implications of central bank policy for the realization of rights must be part of the picture.

Monetary policy today almost universally prioritizes maintaining very low rates of inflation—a goal often referred to as "price stability"—over encouraging economic growth and supporting full employment. Many central banks formalize this policy stance by adopting an approach called "inflation targeting," in which they announce a target range of inflation—for instance, between 1 and 3 percent—and then adjust interest rates and credit supply to try to meet this target (Epstein and Yeldan 2008). Central banks attempt to lower inflation by reducing the growth of credit, dampening demand in the economy, and thereby curtailing upward pressures on prices.

Some economic theories posit that there is no trade-off between lowering inflation and expanding economic activity. They claim that market economies tend to move towards full employment through decentralized decisions of firms and consumers, guided by price signals.[9] Within this theoretical construct, policies that attempt to reduce unemployment below a certain threshold, sometimes called the "natural rate" of unemployment, lead to inflationary pressures.[10] The extent to which lower rates of unemployment actually lead to higher prices depends on a variety of factors, including the determinants of inflation in a particular country, the ways in which prices and wages are set, the degree to which unemployment is a result of slack demand and imperfect markets, and how well labor markets function when matching workers with available job opportunities.

The sources of inflationary pressures must also be taken into account. In many countries, inflation is not primarily caused by central bank policy. In these cases, inflation is not a problem of excessive credit leading to too much demand, but rather a problem of poor infrastructure, low productivity, and the monopoly power of businesses that have sufficient market power to raise prices. Higher prices in global markets for essential goods, such as food and energy, can also contribute to inflation through the cost of imports. Inflation, in other words, can be related to several other issues besides monetary policy.[11] Efforts to contain these non-monetary forms of inflation by contracting the money supply and raising interest rates can have a negative impact on the economy and the realization of rights.

The trade-offs between inflation and employment differ among social groups. As already discussed, monetary policy that tries to reduce inflation by raising interest rates can also reduce employment. However, the costs of losing a job are not distributed equally. More marginalized populations, including women and different ethnic and racial groups, often disproportionately experience the negative consequences of job losses. For example, research has shown that central bank policies adopted during periods of inflation reduction in developing countries have different impacts on women's and men's employment (Braunstein and Heintz 2008). These dynamics need to be taken into account when evaluating monetary policy choices from a human rights perspective.

Central banks can have a key regulatory role with respect to the financial sector, setting out the rules and incentives and determining how the financial sector channels and allocates its resources. By changing these rules, central banks in countries around the world can help mobilize financial resources and channel them to uses that support the realization of rights. For example, central banks could strengthen the regulatory requirements on commercial banks that fail to extend a certain amount of credit to priority areas, for instance housing, job-creating investments, or small-scale loans to the informal self-employed. Positive incentives could also be put in place. If banks are not lending because of perceived risk, government guarantees could be extended on lending to priority areas. Public development banks could also be created, which could be more accountable and interested in facilitating investments that improve the public welfare.

To shield the economy against global shocks, many central banks hold reserves of foreign currency. Foreign exchange reserves are typically denominated in a major international currency, such as the dollar or Euro. In recent decades, the rapid mobility of finance across international borders has increased the risks of financial crises. Short-term inflows of capital—to buy stocks, bonds, and other financial products—can quickly reverse themselves, putting pressure on a country's currency, its financial sector, and the domestic economy. In the event of this kind of rapid outflow of capital, a country can draw on its foreign reserves in order to protect its currency and to provide some insulation against the negative consequences of such a crisis. As a response to the crisis in 1997 in East Asia, many countries in that region began to accumulate large stocks of foreign exchange to serve as a buffer against the rapid mobility of capital.

In many respects, these large stocks of foreign exchange reserves represent idle resources. There are real costs associated with diverting resources towards the accumulation of foreign exchange reserves, instead of using them to finance development (Curz and Walters 2008). From a human rights perspective, the accumulation of reserves could be justified in terms of insuring against a financial crisis that would lead to budget cuts that affect economic and social rights. However, it is important to question whether such safeguards could be secured in other ways, in which case idle reserves could be mobilized for the realization of rights (i.e. they would contribute to the maximum available resources). Explicit restrictions on short-term capital inflows and outflows, often called capital controls, represent one alternative to the accumulation of foreign reserves. By limiting the free movement of capital, particularly financial flows that are speculative in character, countries can open up space to pursue policies that facilitate the realization of basic rights.

In times of crisis, central banks play a pivotal role in supplying financial recourses—e.g. cash—to private financial institutions to prevent a collapse of the financial sector. A central bank is capable of mobilizing enormous amounts of finance to bail out private banks and other financial corporations. For instance, the Federal Reserve, the central bank for the US economy, engaged in a policy of "quantitative easing" during the 2008 financial crisis. Quantitative easing involves injecting significant amounts of cash into the economy by buying up financial assets—such as government bonds and the high risk, questionable assets, such as mortgage-backed securities, that were at the center of the crisis. The Federal Reserve effectively traded cash for assets that were held by private financial institutions.

What happened to all the cash that the financial institutions received? Was it channeled into productive uses that help to prevent a rollback in the enjoyment of rights? The answer is no—the banks just held onto the cash as a kind of insurance policy. Figure 5.1 shows the cash reserves held by banks and other depository institutions at the Federal Reserve from 2001 to 2014. Cash reserves hovered around $20 billion before 2008. With the onset of the crisis, they increased exponentially, exceeding $2.3 trillion

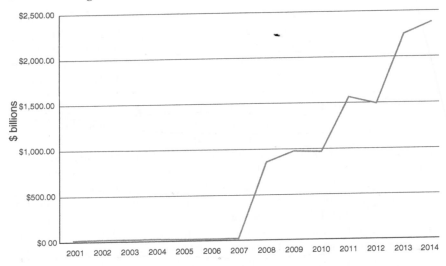

Figure 5.1 Cash reserves of US depository institutions held at the Federal Reserve, 2001–2014

US Federal Reserve Board of Governors (2015)

in 2014. These represent idle reserves in the banking sector that could have been used to support the fulfillment of economic and social rights at a time when those rights were being undermined. The example of the Federal Reserve bailouts raises serious questions about the role of central banks in rescuing financial institutions, the conditions under which these bailouts happen, and the failure to use the maximum available resources to realize basic rights.

Many central banks have a strict price stability mandate under law, with little to no discretion to pursue other policy objectives, such as supporting the realizing of rights. Inflation targeting is often justified in terms of improving the accountability of the central bank, but without an allowance for greater transparency and participation in setting targets and conducting policy. The extent to which the mandate and practices of the central bank, a government institution, fail to address core human rights obligations is not considered. However, there is no reason why central banks should not be held accountable to the same human rights principles as other government organizations.

Conclusion

This chapter has proposed various ways of clarifying, elaborating, and extending the concept of maximum available resources. In so doing, it challenges the approach to maximum available resources that takes as given the broad policy parameters that determine the resources available to support human rights. The mobilization of resources extends to consideration of debt financing, official development assistance, monetary policy in addition to the areas of government spending and taxation discussed in Chapter 4. However, resources are not infinite and the chapter highlights numerous questions that could be raised in the context of evaluating whether a government is using the maximum resources available for the fulfillment of rights. A detailed application of these ideas requires taking into account specific economic, social, and political situations on a country-by-country basis. Nevertheless, the chapter has laid the groundwork for a much more expansive consideration of what it means to use the maximum available resources to realize fundamental human rights.

Notes

1   For further discussion and examples of how these human principles apply, particularly in the case of the US and Mexico, see Balakrishnan and Elson (2011).
2   For an empirical example, see Atukeren (2010).
3   The concepts of odious and illegitimate debt have been recognized in the Guiding Principles (Lumina 2011).
4   For a discussion of odious debt, see Howse (2007).
5   See Zandstra (2011).Two stability mechanisms were used to administer the rescue programs: the European Financial Stability Mechanism and, when more substantial interventions were required, the European Financial Stability Facility.
6   http://www.unmillenniumproject.org/press/07.htm.
7   See, for example, BetterAid (2011). Note: BetterAid merged with the Open Forum for Development Effectiveness to form a new organization, the CSO Partnership for Development Effectiveness.
8   The Millennium Development Goals were adopted in 2000 and provided a partial framework for development until 2015. The post-2015 development agenda refers to what will replace the Millennium Development Goals in terms of goals, targets, and indicators after 2015.
9   The classic exposition of the neoclassical model of market-clearing prices is the Arrow-Debreu model. See Arrow and Debreu (1954).
10 See, for example, Friedman (1968).
11 For a discussion of these issues in the sub-Saharan African context, see Heintz and Ndikumana (2011).

References

Adams, B. and Martens, J. (2015). *Fit for whose purpose? Private funding and corporate influence in the United Nations.* New York: Global Policy Forum.
Arrow, K. and Debreu, G. (1954). Existence of an equilibrium in a competitive economy. *Econometrica* 22(3), pp. 265–90.
Atukeren, E. (2010). Politico-economic determinants of the crowding-in effects of public investments in developing countries. *Journal of Money, Investment, and Banking* 13, pp. 55–74.

Balakrishnan, R. and Elson, D. (2011). Introduction. In: R. Balakrishnan and D. Elson, eds., *Economic Policy and Human Rights: Holding Governments to Account*. London: Zed Books, pp. 1–27.

BetterAid. (2011). Making development cooperation architecture just: Governance principles and pillars. Discussion note from the BetterAid Platform (final version). Available at: http://www.betteraid.org/sites/newbetteraid/files/Making%20development%20cooperation%20just.pdf [Accessed 22 Sept. 2015].

Blundell-Wignall, A. and Slovik, P. (2011). A market perspective on the European sovereign debt and banking crisis. *Financial Market Trends*. pp. 1–28.

Braunstein, E. and Heintz, J. (2008). Gender bias and central bank policy: employment and inflation reduction. *International Review of Applied Economics* 22(2), pp. 173–86.

Clay E., Geddes, M., and Natali, L. (2009). "Aid Untying: Is it Working?" London: Overseas Development Institute.

Curz, M. and Walters, B. (2008). Is the accumulation of international reserves good for development? *Cambridge Journal of Economics* 32, pp. 665–81.

Epstein, G. and Yeldan, E. (2008). Inflation targeting, employment creation and economic development: assessing the impacts and policy alternatives. *International Review of Applied Economics* 22(2), pp. 131–44.

Friedman, M. (1968). The role of monetary policy. *American Economic Review* 58, pp. 1–17.

Guiding Principles on Foreign Debt and Human Rights. (2012). *Report of the Independent Expert on the Effects of Foreign Debt and Other Related International Financial Obligations of States on the Full Enjoyment of All Human Rights, Particularly Economic, Social and Cultural Rights*. A/HRC/20/23. Available at: http://ap.ohchr.org/documents/dpage_e.aspx?si=A/HRC/20/23 [Accessed 26 Sept. 2015].

Heintz, J. (2013). How macroeconomic policy can support economic development in sub-Saharan African Countries. In J. Stiglitz, J. Lin, and E. Patel, eds., *New Thinking on Industrial Policy: Implications for Africa*. New York: Palgrave, pp. 201–15.

Heintz, J. and Ndikumana, L. (2011). Is there a case for inflation targeting in sub-Saharan Africa? *Journal of African Economies* 20, pp. 67–103 (supplement 2).

Howse, R. (2007). *The Concept of Odious Debt in Public International Law*. UNCTAD Discussion Paper 185. Geneva: UNCTAD.

IMF. (2007). *The IMF and Aid to Sub-Saharan Africa*. Evaluation report prepared by the Independent Evaluation Office of the IMF. Washington, DC: IMF.

International Covenant on Economic, Social and Cultural Rights (ICESCR). (1966). Office of the High Commissioner for Human Rights. Available at: http://www.ohchr.org/EN/ProfessionalInterest/Pages/CESCR.aspx [Accessed 26 Sept. 2015].

Lumina, C. (2011). *Report of the Independent Expert on the Effects of Foreign Debt and Other Related International Financial Obligations of States on the Full Enjoyment of All Human Rights, Particularly Economic, Social and Cultural Rights*. A/HRC/17/37. Available at: http://daccess-dds-ny.un.org/doc/UNDOC/GEN/G11/126/15/PDF/G1112615.pdf?OpenElement [Accessed 26 Sept. 2015].

Maxwell, S. (2015). *Financing for Development: A Rapid Assessment.* Available at: http://www.simonmaxwell.eu/blog/financing-for-development-a-rapid-assessment.html [Accessed 18 Sept. 2015].

Muchhala, B. (2015). Opinion: Third FfD Conference fails to finance development—Part One. Available at: http://www.ipsnews.net/2015/07/opinion-third-ffd-conference-fails-to-finance-development-part-one/ [Accessed 18 Sept. 2015].

Regions Refocus, Third World Network, Development Alternatives and Women for a New Era (2015). A geopolitical analysis of financing for development (FfD3). Available at: http://www.twn.my/title2/finance/2015/fi150302/A%20Geopolitical%20Analysis%20of%20FfD3%20-%20Regions%20Refocus,%20TWN,%20DAWN.pdf [Accessed 18 Sept. 2015].

United Nations Declaration on the Right to Development. (1986). Resolution 41/128. Available at: http://www.un.org/documents/ga/res/41/a41r128.htm [Accessed 26 Sept. 2015].

United Nations Development Program. (2011). *Towards Human Resilience: Sustaining MDG Progress in an Age of Economic Uncertainty.* New York: UNDP. Available at: http://www.undp.org/content/dam/undp/library/Poverty%20Reduction/Towards_SustainingMDG_Web1005.pdf [Accessed 18 Sept. 2015].

UN Women. (2015). *Progress of the World's Women 2015–16. Transforming Economies, Realizing Rights.* New York: UN Women. Available at: http://progress.unwomen.org/en/2015/pdf/UNW_progressreport.pdf [Accessed 18 Sept. 2015].

US Federal Reserve Board of Governors. (2015). *Financial Accounts of the United States.* Data download. Data release 11 June 2015. Available at: http://www.federalreserve.gov/datadownload/Choose.aspx?rel=Z.1 [Accessed 16 Sept. 2015].

World Bank Group (2013). *Financing for Development: Post 2015.* Washington, DC: World Bank Group.

Zandstra, D. (2011).The European sovereign debt crisis and its evolving resolution. *Capital Markets Law Journal* 6(3), pp. 285–316.

6 Financialization, credit markets, and human rights[1]

The influence of financial interests has expanded significantly in the decades since the 1980s, a time of far-reaching changes to the regulatory environment that has altered the landscape of global economic governance. The ascendency of financial markets has enormous implications for the realization of rights. To give just one example, the 2008 financial crisis led to record unemployment rates, home foreclosures, cutbacks to government expenditures, and rising levels of poverty in the US economy. The damage was not limited to one country or region. The financial meltdown sent shockwaves to other economies, with similar disastrous results. The choices global financial institutions made were directly responsible for the crisis, yet many revisionist arguments in the wake of the meltdown have assigned responsibility to the reckless behavior of borrowers—including the individuals holding subprime mortgages and governments in peripheral countries. Financial firms enjoyed sizable bailouts, while others were left to shoulder the burden of adjustment.

This chapter explores the role of financial institutions and credit markets in shaping the environment within which rights are realized or, in many cases, rolled back. Both financial fragility and policy responses to economic crises are shaped by power dynamics in financial markets that interact with existing structures of stratification along the lines of race, gender, nationality, and other group differences. These dynamics are not unique to the 2008 global economic catastrophe and have been evident in other economic crises. Despite the centrality of financial markets in contributing to economic instability, controls on financial institutions have been loosened in recent years rather than tightened, indicating that policy regimes are tilted towards the interest of finance rather than the fulfillment of basic rights. Moreover, the process of financialization means that financial incentives, motives, and dynamics affect the markets for non-financial goods and services in ways that undermine the realization of human rights. For example, this chapter examines the role financial speculation in commodity futures markets played in pushing up global food prices during 2005–2007, threatening millions of people's right to food.

Finance, power, and inequality

Over the past four decades, countries around the world have experienced a process of "financialization"—the growing dominance of finance in the economy and in people's lives. There are many definitions of what is meant by financialization—from the growing size of the financial sector in national economies to a shift in the composition of profits away from earnings generated from productive activities towards those generated through speculative financial investments. For the purposes of this discussion, we follow Gerald Epstein (2006)[2] in adopting a broad interpretation of financialization, defining it in terms of the increasing dominance of financial motives, financial institutions (including financial markets), and financial interests in national and global economies. The process of financialization has been associated with fundamental changes to the regulatory environment that has limited the scope for government intervention in financial markets. Financial institutions exert a strong influence over economic governance and the direction of policy. This raises important questions of what can be done to change how finance is regulated to avoid the negative consequences of financialization for the realization of rights.

Profits earned from financial activities are referred to as rents—a term used by economists to mean income secured by controlling scarce resources. Unlike other scarce resources that earn rents, such as natural resources, modern financial assets are not backed by a physical commodity, and as a result their scarcity is socially constructed—based on monetary policy decisions, the structure of financial institutions, and the regulatory environment. Rentiers, those who control scarce financial resources, are able to stake a claim on the income produced in the rest of the economy. The dominance of rentier interests is a central feature of financialized economies.

Credit markets are a particularly important subset of financial markets. Credit markets refer to those exchanges and contractual agreements in which lenders provide borrowers with access to current funds in exchange for a claim on future streams of income or revenues. The power relationship in credit markets is derived from these claims on future income combined with the ability of those on the short-side of the market to sanction the other party in exchanges (Bowles and Gintis 1993). Creditors typically represent the short-side of the market, since they control access to scarce financial resources in a context in which demand for loans frequently exceeds supply. The threat of withholding access to financial resources, and the ability to demand repayment on specified terms, serves as an effective sanction and gives lenders power over borrowers. Debt becomes a disciplinary device that can be used to control individual behavior, shape government policy, reinforce global dependencies, and restructure economies.

The fact that borrowers are perceived to have voluntarily entered into credit agreements is often used to argue that they are responsible for any negative consequences arising from the loan. After all, they could have chosen not to have taken out a loan. However, this line of reasoning ignores the creditor's role and the existence of unequal power dynamics, even when borrowers freely choose to take on debt (Bowles and Gintis 1993). The choice to enter into a credit agreement may not be freely chosen if, for example, the refusal to borrow would be associated with more dire consequences (i.e. the effective bankruptcy of a country). If we consider the case of the subprime mortgage crisis, the meaning of "free choice" becomes questionable when loans were made in the context of outright fraud.[3]

It is not always profitable for creditors to withhold credit. Lenders, in an effort to boost profitability, create new markets, often extending loans to borrowers or groups previously excluded from credit markets, although on less favorable terms. The expansion of credit and the creation of new markets are mutually reinforcing processes, as theorized by post-Keynesian economists such as Hyman Minsky (1986). Many post-Keynesian theories argue that credit expansion during good times supports investment and growth, leading to strong profits, higher levels of spending, and rising asset values—all of which encourage the extension of still more credit. However, these dynamics lead to a buildup of debt, which eventually produces conditions of economic fragility.

Fragility arises from the growing claims of creditors in terms of interest and loan repayments relative to the income available to borrowers. In a highly indebted, fragile economy, a shock to incomes and revenue streams can quickly precipitate a crisis (Minsky 1986). Borrowers who are no longer able to meet their obligations default on their loans. Moreover, when a crisis occurs, credit dries up and creates a situation in which lenders are able to exercise a significant degree of power over borrowers. Financial institutions are able to protect their interests by this exercise of power, thereby shifting the burden of adjusting to a crisis onto less powerful groups in ways that reinforce existing social stratifications. In this process, the responsibility for the crisis is assigned to the borrowers— often portrayed as reckless, profligate, or naive.

Many economists see credit and financial markets as operating at the macroeconomic level and therefore having little to do with inequality. In reality, these markets interact with institutions and structures that reflect power inequalities along the lines of race, gender, class, and nation.[4] Changes at the macroeconomic level—such as a credit boom or a financial crisis—produce outcomes that reflect existing social stratifications. Economic shocks frequently have long-run consequences, which suggests that, when the costs of adjusting to changes in the macroeconomic environment are unevenly distributed, economic crises contribute to the persistence of patterns of stratification.[5]

For instance, an empirical study by Stephanie Seguino and James Heintz (2012) found that policy decisions taken by the US Federal Reserve to raise interest rates have a disproportionately negative effect on the unemployment rate of blacks relative to that of white males and on the unemployment rate of women relative to white males. These racial and gender distinctions in the response to macroeconomic policies vary across different US states, with the relative importance of race and gender linked to the racial composition of each state's population. This suggests that variations in the nature of inequalities between social groups shape the distributive consequences of macroeconomic policy.

Collective action among dominant groups secures their material advantages and facilitates the reproduction of social stratification over time.[6] The construction of identities of "whiteness," masculinity, and nationality facilitate such collective action. Scholars have theorized that the emergence and persistence of race and gender identities are sensitive to the economic benefits of maintaining those identities (Darity et al. 2006). During an economic downturn, when jobs become scarce and household resources come under pressure, the relative benefits of maintaining identities associated with dominant, privileged groups may increase, leading to more pronounced racist, patriarchal, and nationalist practices. For instance, Greece experienced an increase in racial and xenophobic violence as a result of economic downturn associated with the austerity policies the country adopted following the 2008 global financial crisis (UNHC 2010). At the same time, economic theories often ignore the importance of collective identities. These alternative explanations of the existence of intergroup disparities tend to locate the reasons for persistent inequalities in personal failings, a lack of individual responsibility, insufficient human capital, genetics, or behaviors linked to cultural differences.

Similar dynamics are evident at the global level. Powerful nations secure their advantages in the global economy in ways that replicate international inequalities and construct national collective identities that reward their citizens with concrete benefits—such as higher standards of living. Outside the countries that dominate the global economy, economic crises are often explained by an inability of governments to manage their economies effectively. The global financial system exhibits inequalities that mirror the international distribution of income and power. The dollar remains the dominant global currency, giving the United States a structural advantage in international transactions. When other countries run into problems paying for imported goods and servicing their foreign debt, access to an international currency becomes critically important. Under these circumstances, many countries must borrow, often from international financial institutions like the International Monetary Fund (IMF). The United States does not face these constraints, having access to an abundant source of dollars.

However, even the US faces limits in global financial markets. Someone must be willing to hold dollars, and most recently, countries such as China and Korea have taken on this role, building up large stocks of foreign exchange reserves (see also Chapter 5). This produces a particular balance of power in the global economy between large debtors (e.g. the United States) and large creditors (e.g. China). Stephen S. Cohen and J. Bradford DeLong stress this point regarding the global balance of financial power with the following illustration: "If you owe the bank $1 million, the bank has you; if you owe $1 billion, you have the bank" (2010, p. 5). While China's economy exerts influence over the US economy, smaller and less influential countries face significant constraints with regard to what their governments can and cannot do, due to these inequalities within global financial markets.

Subprime mortgages: debt, inequality, and economic instability

Prior to the 2008 financial crisis, credit had been made readily available in the US economy through mortgage loans to buy houses, credit cards to purchase consumer goods and services, and other forms of credit, such as home equity loans, to finance a range of expenditures. Availability of credit and household indebtedness have increased significantly since the early 1980s. According to the Flow of Funds Accounts released by the Federal Reserve Board of Governors, household debt averaged 65 percent of personal disposable income from 1960 to 1979.[7] Since the 1980s, household indebtedness began to increase and grew to 132 percent of disposable income in 2007—the year before the global financial crisis.

Despite this expansion in the availability of credit at the aggregate level over recent decades, access to credit had been circumscribed by race and gender. Specifically, discriminatory lending practices marginalized racial groups in credit and housing markets (Dymski 2006). With the expansion of subprime mortgages, that is, mortgages that require less up-front cash and lower incomes than standard mortgages, these patterns of exclusion from credit markets changed. Credit began to be extended to previously excluded populations, although on unfavorable terms. Women and people of color were particularly targeted in US credit markets. This allowed historically unprecedented access to housing markets, although at higher costs than for standard mortgages. Subprime lending represented a lucrative new market opportunity for creditors.

Two studies, both by Fishbein and Woodall (2006a and 2006b), for the Consumer Federation of America examined the race and gender dimensions of subprime mortgage lending. The studies found that about 24 percent of male borrowers received subprime mortgages compared with about 32 percent of female borrowers. They also found discrimination between different racial and ethnic groups: about 20 percent of white borrowers and 13.5 percent of Asian borrowers received subprime loans in 2005, compared with almost 40 percent of Latino borrowers and over 50 percent of African American borrowers. African American women were

5.7 percent more likely to receive a subprime mortgage than African American men, and 256 percent more likely to receive one than white men. The costs of a subprime mortgage relative to a standard mortgage were substantial. Subprime borrowers were estimated to pay between $85,000 and $186,000 more in interest than average borrowers over the period of a typical mortgage.

Through the growth of credit, people in the United States appeared to be experiencing an expansion in access to economic goods and services. Average hourly wages, adjusted for inflation, had been stagnant in the United States for decades. According to data from the US Bureau of Labor Statistics, the hourly wage of production for nonsupervisory workers, measured in 2007 dollars, was $18.08/hour in 1970 and $17.81/hour in 2007—the year before the major effects of the financial crisis became known.[8] Household incomes increased, even taking into account inflation, but this was due to longer hours worked by all household members, explained in large part by women's increased labor force participation. Income inequality between households grew significantly during this period, but growth of consumer demand of low-income households was sustained by a rapid growth in household indebtedness, which helped lay the foundation for the economic crisis (Reich 2011).

Debts have to be repaid at some point, but the rising prices of houses led many to feel secure because rising prices made individuals wealthier, given prevailing asset values. These wealth effects help explain expansions in the general demand for credit. Higher asset prices meant that households found their wealth was increasing without having to save, allowing for more borrowing without diminishing their net worth (the total value of assets owned less what is owed).

The subprime mortgage crisis—and the broader financial crisis—was triggered by an abrupt change in this economic environment interacting with the fragile situation created by large amounts of debt. The US Federal Reserve provided an impetus for the collapse of the housing bubble by dramatically raising its key interest rate, the Federal Funds rate, from a low of 1.1 per cent in 2003 to 5 percent by 2006. Interest rates had been lowered during the 2001 recession and were later raised due to concerns over modest increases in inflation. The subprime mortgages were not fixed-rate mortgages. Instead, monthly payments were tied to market interest rates. When the Federal Reserve raised its interest rate by a multiple of over four times the low rates that had prevailed during the height of the boom, monthly payments on subprime loans quickly became unaffordable. Defaults became commonplace, and the housing market collapsed.

The collapse of the housing market created ripple effects throughout the global financial sector. Financial institutions had been investing in various financial instruments whose ultimate value was linked to the mortgage markets. Mortgages were bundled in a process called "securitization" and then repackaged to produce new, innovative financial products.[9] The complexities of these products prevented any accurate assessment of risk. However, they did create an environment of economic fragility that was much more substantial than that associated with the subprime mortgage market alone.

The previously marginalized borrowers who were disproportionately represented in the subprime mortgage markets also suffered disproportionately from the negative fallout from the collapse of the housing market. According to a report from the Center for Responsible Lending, approximately 25 percent of African American and Latino borrowers who took out loans from 2004 to 2008 lost their homes to foreclosure or were seriously delinquent by February 2011, compared with just under 12 percent of white borrowers (Bocian et al. 2011).

In contrast, financial institutions were bailed out, in part through the federal budget and the Troubled Asset Relief Program (TARP), and much more significantly through the actions of the Federal Reserve, which bought up questionable assets linked to the subprime mortgage market (General Accountability Office 2011; 2009).[10] While the original federal rescue package (TARP) was meant to include provisions for preserving home ownership and providing mortgage debt relief, in reality the funds were only distributed to help financial institutions (Barofsky 2011).[11] The bailouts were justified on the grounds that failures of large financial institutions posed a serious threat to the US economy. The implication was that mortgage defaults by African Americans, Latinos, and women in low-income households represented an isolated risk with few implications for those not directly involved.

Stepping back from the details of the rise and fall of the subprime mortgage market, we find that the policy response appears to have treated the large financial players as if they were "blameless victims" deserving of government intervention and not held responsible for decisions made. In contrast, subprime borrowers received far less support—consistent with the perspective that they were responsible for the defaults and foreclosures, having made unwise, unsustainable, and risky choices. The contrast in the image of the systemically important investment banker (white, mostly male, privileged, shrewd) and the "typical" subprime mortgage borrower (nonwhite, poor, female, and reckless) is mirrored in the policy response.[12] The role of credit in the crisis is fundamental, as is the way in which power is distributed through credit markets. In the midst of the crisis, both subprime borrowers and major investment banks were holding large amounts of debts and assets with questionable value, but the relative vulnerability of the two groups was dramatically different.

Latin America's debt crisis and capital flight from Africa

The economic and power dynamics associated with the subprime mortgage crisis and the ensuing global financial crisis have been evident elsewhere. In many respects, the subprime mortgage and sovereign debt crises are typical, rather than exceptional, with regard to how these scenarios play out. To see this, it is worth taking a look at some additional examples not tied to this recent financial crisis: the Latin American debt crisis of the 1980s and capital flight from sub-Saharan Africa.

The oil shocks of the 1970s had significant negative consequences for the global economy and for many countries in Latin America. At the same time, credit was readily available—that is, there was excess liquidity in global markets, meaning that there was an abundant supply of credit looking for markets (Pastor 1989). Borrowing by Latin American governments increased significantly in the 1970s and the very early 1980s. However, changes in global credit markets, partly because of dramatic shifts in monetary policies in countries like the United States, meant that easy credit was no longer available beginning in the early 1980s. Many Latin American countries found that they could no longer finance their public debts. High global interest rates added to this problem. Several large Latin American countries, including Brazil, Argentina, and Mexico, faced sovereign debt crises of their own.

The Latin American debt crisis raised the specter of contagion and serious systemic risks for global markets and financial interests outside the region (Felix 1990). For these reasons, stabilization packages were initiated by the International Monetary Fund (IMF) and the United States in an attempt to rescue Latin American financial institutions. For instance, the US Brady Plan involved the issuance of bonds, backed by guarantees that would replace bank loans made to Latin American countries and thereby relieve some of the pressures created by the large debts (Ibid.). Loans from the IMF were subject to conditionalities that involved spending cuts, significant devaluation of currencies, and limits on wages in an attempt to control inflation (Ibid.). The burden of adjustment primarily fell on the borrowers. Moreover, the Latin American debt crisis represented a watershed in the history of the IMF, in the sense that it gave the IMF significant power over the governance of economies in Latin America.

As with the subprime mortgage crisis, the mainstream narrative that emerged out of the Latin American debt crisis was one of overborrowing, policy mistakes, and macroeconomic mismanagement on the part of the Latin American countries (Felix 1990). The question of overlending and financial institutions' responsibility for the crisis were not reflected in the policy response. Once again, in this narrative, the banks effectively became the victims of the irresponsible behavior of reckless borrowers. The negative consequences of the debt crisis and the policy conditionalities were substantial—declining per capita incomes, high rates of unemployment, falling wages, and a collapse of investment (Ibid.).

The second example of these kinds of credit market dynamics is that of debt-financed capital flight from sub-Saharan Africa. Léonce Ndikumana and James Boyce (2011) have documented the extent of capital flight and its relationship to debt in a large number of sub-Saharan African countries. In their work, capital flight is defined as unrecorded financial flows out of a country—that is, flows not related to trade, foreign investment, interest payments, or external borrowing. Political and economic elites in many African countries have moved large amounts of money out of their countries, converting this money into personal assets, such as bank accounts or other investments. These outflows of finance are unrecorded— and therefore constitute a sizable share of what Ndikumana and Boyce refer to as capital flight. They show that many sub-Saharan African countries are net creditors to the rest of the world. In other words, taking capital flight into account, financial flows out of African countries to the rest of the world have exceeded inflows.

Ndikumana and Boyce find a relationship between external borrowing and capital flight in many sub-Saharan African countries (2011). This suggests that borrowing facilitates capital flight, and the resources that enter a country in the form of loans can leave the country in the form of capital flight. Political and economic elites become richer while debt burdens grow. This debt must be serviced, placing pressures on government expenditures and generating real human costs in terms of lack of basic medical care, curtailed access to education, and lower levels of public services (Ibid.).

Like the other examples of debt and credit markets, the debt burden of African countries is often said to be the result of macroeconomic mismanagement and excessive borrowing. In some respects this is true. Given the existence of capital flight and considering the ultimate destination of the funds, borrowing could certainly be said to have been excessive. The African political and economic elites who benefited from capital flight are portrayed as corrupt, enriching themselves at the expense of the rest of the population. These narratives are based on the actual experiences of many countries (Ndikumana and Boyce 2011). However, what is often missing from the story is the role of the international banks and financial institutions, usually based in the global north, whose cooperation was essential in order for capital flight to take place. These financial institutions facilitate capital flight because it is profitable to do so. In addition, they protect the assets and the identities of the elites in African countries who are responsible for capital flight. Yet the role of these institutions is often ignored, and the responsibility for the debt burden is racialized—that is, portrayed only in terms of corrupt and uncivilized behavior that is assumed to be characteristic of underdevelopment in Africa.

As the debt of sub-Saharan African countries became unsustainable, they were often subject to similar rescue packages with similar conditionalities to those imposed on Latin America. The debt situation in these sub-Saharan African countries was deemed dire enough to create a new label for them: "heavily indebted poor countries," or HIPCs. Again, the burden of adjustment fell on the borrowers. In the case of capital flight from the sub-Saharan African countries, the requirement that the borrowing country bear the primary burden is particularly unjust—the consequences of debt are borne by the general population, while collaboration between political elites and overseas financial institutions yielded large benefits for those directly involved in moving money out of the countries.

Financialization and the right to food

Financial markets can have spillover effects in other markets in ways that affect the realization of specific rights. As markets become increasingly financialized, financial incentives, motivations, and dynamics can alter basic prices in ways that have little to do with actual production and the demand for the goods being traded. One example is the financialization of commodity markets and its connection to the global food crisis that emerged in 2005 to 2007. The rise in speculative activity by financial investors has been linked to a dramatic increase in the price of basic commodities in ways that undermined the right to food (De Schutter 2010).

A wide range of commodities exhibited dramatic price increases during the first decade of the twenty-first century—including the prices of food commodities and energy commodities with important implications. Figure 6.1 shows a commodity price index, constructed by the International Monetary Fund, capturing the average price level across a broad range of commodities from January 1993 to April 2012. Prices began to rise beginning around 2002–2003 and peaked in 2008 immediately before the global financial crisis unfolded later that year. Although prices fell with the onset of the crisis, they recovered quickly and, by 2012, returned to levels similar to those that prevailed immediately before the financial collapse.[13] The global impact of these price hikes prior to the 2008 financial crisis were enormous—an additional 75 million people were estimated to suffer from hunger and 105 million were estimated to have experienced extreme poverty because of the higher prices (Abbott 2009). The impact on those who were already poor and hungry prior to the crisis was catastrophic.

The price increases were not restricted to a single market or a small subset of markets. The boom of the 2000s was evident across a variety of commodities—agricultural products, precious metals, and energy. These bubble-like dynamics generated a great deal of debate over the causes of the increase in commodity prices. One explanation is that the trading

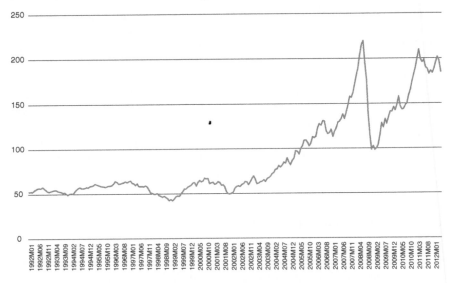

Figure 6.1 IMF Commodity Price Index (all commodities), Jan. 1992–May 2012
International Monetary Fund (2015)

activity of financial investors contributed to the rise in prices (UNCTAD 2009; 2011). Over this period, investors moved into commodity futures markets and began to hold diversified portfolios of contracts. The increase in financial investments in these markets—a form of financialization— was reflected in a rapid rise in the trading activity, as indicated by growing level of open interest (i.e. the number of outstanding futures contracts at a particular point in time). Figure 6.2 charts the increase in open interest in commodity futures contracts over the same time period presented in Figure 6.1.[14] The correlation between the number of outstanding futures contracts and the average price level across commodities is striking.

New types of investment products encouraged investment in commodity futures markets. For example, index funds were created to allow individuals and institutions to effectively invest in a broad range of commodity futures.[15] Index funds are types of investments linked to commodity price indices produced by financial institutions, such as the Standard and Poor's-Goldman Sachs commodity index and the Dow Jones-UBS index. Typically, returns on investments in index funds would increase when prices increase. In effect, these new types of investment products allowed financial markets to bet on future commodity price increases.

Where did these new financial products come from? Diversified portfolios of certain investments in commodity futures had been shown to produce returns roughly equivalent to those of stock markets, but the returns would be negatively correlated with share prices (see Erb and Harvey 2006; Gorton and Rouwenhorst 2006). Investments in commodity

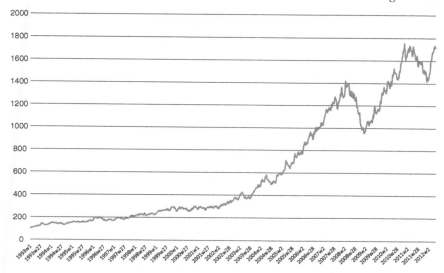

Figure 6.2 Index of open interest, weekly, Jan. 1993–April 2012
Commodity Futures Trading Commission (2015)

futures, if sufficiently diversified, could therefore provide an alternative investment to traditional stock markets for financiers. Broad trends in financial investment from the 1990s to 2008 reveal that investors moved from one type of financial investment to the next. The 1990s was the decade for equities, with the so-called "dot com" bubble. With the 2001 recession, investors began to diversify, moving into real estate and the mortgage-backed securities that were at the root of the 2008 financial crisis. Finally, in the mid-2000s, the movement into commodity futures began in earnest. The increase in investment in futures markets could lead to an increase in futures prices if there were an increasing number of people betting on an increase in commodity prices in the future.

Investors in commodity futures can take either a "short" or a "long" position. With a short position, the person holding the futures contract agrees to sell the underlying commodity at a specified price at a particular time in the future. Short positions are often adopted as a kind of insurance against price declines—for example, farmers may adopt short positions in futures markets to lock in a price for their crop in the future. With a long position, the person holding the contract agrees to buy the underlying commodity at a specified price in the future. People who adopt long positions expect commodity prices to rise in the future.

Many of the financial investors in commodity futures leading up to the price spikes in food and energy prices had adopted long positions. In other words, they were betting that commodity prices would increase in the future. With large numbers of investors taking long positions in the markets, futures prices increased and these price increases were then transmitted to the actual prices of commodities—wheat, corn, petroleum, natural gas, copper, and so on. Therefore, speculation on commodity futures markets provides a channel through which financial investment can affect the price of food.

The exact magnitude of the effect of speculative investment on food and energy prices remains a matter of debate (Ghosh, Heintz, and Pollin 2012). Nevertheless, the dramatic increase in financial investments in commodity futures markets appears to have played a role in the food and energy price hikes over this period. Financial investors and institutions therefore have the potential to distort prices in other markets in ways that undermine the realization of human rights. One implication of this kind of financialization of non-financial markets is that the role of financial players in influencing the prices of basic goods should be scrutinized much more than it currently is and regulatory interventions should be introduced to prevent the rollback of economic and social rights.

Why human rights matters for financialization

The contribution of financial markets to these economic crises raises serious concerns over how these markets are currently governed. Finance does not operate in a vacuum, independently of the rest of society and the economy. The financial crises and related phenomena discussed in this chapter come at a high cost, the costs are unequally distributed, and they are intricately linked to how credit markets operate. The human rights approach provides a set of obligations and principles that represent an alternative approach to regulating finance. There has been relatively little dialogue between those working within the framework of human rights and those analyzing various aspects of macroeconomic governance.[16] Throughout this book, we have shown how certain concepts coming from the human rights framework, with specific attention on economic and social rights, have potentially far-reaching implications for the way in which economic policies are formulated, and this applies to financial markets as well.

The basic human rights obligations and principles were discussed in detail in Chapter 2 and have been elaborated throughout this book. In this chapter, we focus on the following:

- the obligation to protect—requires the state to take steps in order to protect rights from actions by third parties that interfere with the enjoyment of those rights;
- the principles of progressive realization and non-retrogression—the state must take steps to progressively realize economic and social rights over time and to prevent an erosion of those rights;
- the principle of maximum available resources—requires the state to undertake steps to use the maximum of available resources to progressively realize economic and social rights;

- the principle of non-discrimination and equality—the state must ensure the equal enjoyment of rights in terms of both its conduct and the outcomes of its policies. Because of the focus on substantive outcomes, "race blind" or "gender blind" policies are not sufficient for compliance with this principle. Non-discrimination also implies that positive steps must be taken to reduce already existing inequalities;
- the principle of accountability, participation, and transparency—governments are obliged to provide mechanisms through which people can hold the state accountable, can participate in policy-making, and can access the information required to do so.

Compliance with these obligations and principles constitutes a very different approach to regulating financial markets and responding to crises when compared to the approach that dominated policy-making over the past several decades. For instance, has deregulation of financial markets allowed global investors to make decisions that led to the 2008 global financial crisis? The outcome of the crisis in many countries has been a retrogression of economic and social rights, which is discussed in greater detail in Chapter 8. This represents a failure of the obligation to protect. The lack of any systematic mortgage regulation in the US markets, which allowed predatory lending to flourish, also represents a failure with regard to the obligation to protect and, given the demographics of those caught up in the subprime mortgage crisis, a violation of the principle of non-discrimination and equality. Similarly, the use of resources by governments and central banks to bail out financial institutions and the subsequent imposition of austerity budgets without demanding greater accountability of the rescued banks and investment firms could be said to violate the principle of maximum available resources as well as the principles of accountability, participation, and transparency.

Moreover, the principle of maximum available resources could be used to justify reform that requires financial institutions to support the progressive realization of economic rights, since the "available resources" include the credit and monetary system, as discussed in Chapter 5. This could be achieved, for example, by requiring banks to provide credit to populations shut out of financial services on favorable terms or by regulating the extension of credit so that a portion of loans support affordable housing, health care facilities, or investments that generate jobs in areas of high unemployment. Recognition of economic and social rights as entitlements that the state must respect, protect, and fulfill would alter the power dynamics of credit markets. These rights extend beyond a narrow focus on property rights, which form the institutional foundation of market economies. We have argued that the asymmetries of power in credit and financial markets have been responsible for the kind of financial crises we have witnessed and the dramatically uneven consequences of those crises. The human rights framework suggests a fundamentally different approach to financial governance that begins to address these concerns.

Of course, the actual implementation of the human rights principles and obligations is more difficult. There is a tension between the capacity of individual states to take steps to support the realization of economic and social rights and the dynamics of an integrated global economy in which financial interests have significant power. Under these conditions, coordinated action by states, including government agencies like central banks, will need to fully support the core principles and obligations discussed here. To give a concrete example, how financial markets in the United States are regulated has implications for realizing economic and social rights elsewhere. If this framework is to move beyond a focus on the nation-state and to recognize the need for action globally, a number of conditions must be met. Countries should not be able to opt out of their human rights obligations. Global and international institutions must be accountable to the same set of human rights obligations as individual governments. The obligations that states have with regard to other countries need to be much better defined, explicitly recognizing power differentials in the global economy. Effective mechanisms for coordination across countries must be developed, including the creation of a common set of rules for regulating transnational businesses and financial players. These issues are explored in greater detail in Chapter 7.

Conclusion

In many respects, debt and credit markets lie at the core of the agglomeration of financial markets and institutions that have become increasingly influential in recent decades: directly influencing the paths that economies take, determining—to a large extent—the policies adopted and limiting the scope for advancements in social justice. We have argued that the operation of these markets reflects inherent power relationships that interact with existing patterns of stratification, producing mainstream discourses that hide unequal racial and gender dynamics and reshape policy responses. These features of financial markets are not unique to the 2008 collapse and can be found in numerous other economic disasters that have occurred in the current era of global financialization, in which policy decisions have intensified, rather than curtailed, the growing power of finance.

The human rights approach has significant potential to turn this situation around. Yet, challenges remain. Perhaps the biggest difficulty with regard to applying this approach to global finance is the need to flesh out how best to coordinate action among states at the global level in ways that take into account unequal power dynamics and support the fulfillment of basic rights. Clearly, the current institutional infrastructure is not sufficiently developed in all dimensions to allow this to happen. Nevertheless, steps can be taken to build on what currently exists and to push out the frontiers of economic governance. For example, revisiting the US subprime mortgage crisis through the lens of human rights reveals a fundamentally different approach to economic governance when compared with the recent dominance of neoliberal policies. There is a long way to go before these alternatives are realized, and it will not happen overnight. If the aim is to progressively realize a new approach to finance, much can be gained through ongoing explorations of the potency, and possible limitations, of the human rights framework.

Notes

1 Portions of this chapter incorporate material from a previously published article. James Heintz and Radhika Balakrishnan. (2012). Debt, Power, and Crisis: Social Stratification and the Inequitable Governance of Financial Markets. *American Quarterly* 64(3), pp. 387–409. © 2012 The American Studies Association. Reprinted with permission of Johns Hopkins University Press.
2 See in particular the Introduction (pp. 3–16).
3 The US Federal Bureau of Investigation recognized the existence of widespread mortgage fraud in the United States during the period in which the subprime mortgage market was expanding rapidly. See: http://www.fbi.gov/news/stories/2008/january/fin_fradu013108 [Accessed 16 Sept. 2015].
4 Inequalities between socially constructed groups are often referred to as horizontal inequalities. See Chapter 3 for a more detailed discussion.
5 This can happen when the shocks associated with a crisis period have long-run consequences. For example, episodes of unemployment have been shown to negatively affect future earnings (see Arulampalam 2001). Similarly, transitions into the labor market during bad economic times appear to have long-term effects on career paths (see Kahn 2010).
6 Mills (1999) uses the concept of a "racial contract," in contrast to the "social contract" construct of contractarian social theory and ethics, to describe forms of collective action among whites that promote their collective interests and subordinate those who are not white. See also Darity (2005).
7 The Flow of Funds Accounts are produced by the US Federal Reserve and contain estimates of financial assets and liabilities for various sectors of the US economy. For more details, see http:// www.federalreserve.gov/apps/fof/ [Accessed 16 Sept. 2015].
8 See www.bls.gov. Hourly wages were inflation-adjusted using the consumer price index for all urban consumers. Estimates of hourly wages came from the Bureau of Labor Statistics' Current Employment Survey program.
9 Financial products directly linked to mortgages were called "mortgage-backed securities" or "asset-backed securities." The "collateralized debt obligations," or CDOs, represented one form of mortgage-backed security. Other financial products, such as "credit default swaps," effectively acted as insurance policies in the event of a default on debt.
10 According to a story published by *Bloomberg Markets* magazine on 27 November 2011, based on the analysis of documents obtained through a Freedom of Information request, the Federal Reserve had committed $7.7 trillion to bail out the financial system by March 2009. Available at: http:// www.bloomberg.com/news/2011-11-28/secret-fed-loans-undisclosed-to-congress-gave-banks-13-billion-in-income.html [Accessed 25 Sept. 2015].
11 Neil M. Barofsky was the special inspector general for the Troubled Asset Relief Program.

12 In reality, white borrowers accounted for a significantly larger absolute number of foreclosures and delinquencies than African American or Latino borrowers (Bocian et al. 2011).
13 At the time of writing, the IMF all commodity price index had begun to fall in the second half of 2014 and is currently below the peak levels of the food and energy crisis prior to the 2008 financial crisis. Lower petroleum prices contributed to the decline in the index.
14 The index of open interest takes on a value of 100 for the first week in January, 1993. The aggregate index of open interest was constructed as a weighted geometric mean across the individual futures markets for each commodity. The weights used were based on the total value of the commodities underlying each contract using current market values for the commodity in question. The weights represent the total market value of the commodities represented by the open interest in each individual market divided by the total market value of commodities across all markets.
15 The returns to investments in index funds are linked to movements in the underlying price index. Individual investors in index funds are actually not investing in futures markets directly. However, the financial institutions that manage the index funds will take a position in the actual commodity futures markets. It is through this mechanism that the growth of index funds led to growth in investments in commodity futures contracts.
16 For a much more detailed examination of the relationship between economic and social rights and macroeconomic policy, see Balakrishnan and Elson (2011).

References

Abbott, P. (2009). *Development Dimensions of Higher Food Prices*. OECD Food, Agriculture, and Fisheries Working Paper. No. 18. Paris: OECD.
Arulampalam, W. (2001). Is unemployment really scarring? Effects of unemployment experiences on wages. *Economic Journal* 111, pp. 585–606.
Balakrishnan, R. and Elson, D. (2011). Introduction. In: R. Balakrishnan and D. Elson, eds., *Economic Policy and Human Rights: Holding Governments to Account*. London: Zed Press, pp. 1–27.
Barofsky, N. M. (2011). Where the bailout went wrong. *New York Times*, 29 March 2011. Available at: http://www.nytimes.com/2011/03/30/opinion/30barofsky.html [Accessed 29 Sept. 2015].
Bocian, D. G., Li, W., Reid, C., and Quercia, R. (2011). *Lost Ground 2011: Disparities in Mortgage Lending and Foreclosures*. Durham, NC: Center for Responsible Lending.
Bowles, S. and Gintis, H. (1993). The revenge of homo economicus: Contested exchange and the revival of political economy. *Journal of Economic Perspectives* 7(1), pp. 83–102.
Cohen, S. S. and DeLong, J. B. (2010). *The End of Influence: What Happens When Other Countries Have the Money*. New York: Basic Books.
Commodity Futures Trading Commission. (2015). Commitment of Traders data. Available at: http://www.cftc.gov/MarketReports/CommitmentsofTraders/index.htm [Accessed 27 Nov. 2015].
Darity, W. (2005). Stratification economics: The role of intergroup inequality. *Journal of Economics and Finance* 29(2), pp. 144–53.

Darity, W., Mason, P., and Stewart, J. (2006). The economics of identity: The origin and persistence of racial norms. *Journal of Economic Behavior and Organizations* 60(3), pp. 283–305.

De Schutter, O. (2010). *Food Commodities Speculation and Food Price Crises: Regulation to Reduce the Risks of Price Volatility.* Briefing Note 2. September. Geneva: Office of the High Commissioner for Human Rights. Available at: www2.ohchr. org/english/issues/food/docs/Briefing_Note_02_September_2010_EN.pdf [Accessed 29 Sept. 2015].

Dymski, G. (2006). Discrimination in the credit and housing markets: Findings and challenges. In: W. M. Rodgers, ed., *Handbook on the Economics of Discrimination.* Cheltenham, UK: Elgar, pp. 215–59.

Epstein, G. (2006). *Financialization and the World Economy.* Northampton, MA: Edward Elgar Publishers.

Erb, C. B. and Harvey, C. R. (2006). The strategic and tactical value of commodity futures. *Financial Analysts Journal* 62(2), pp. 69–97.

Felix, D. (1990). Latin America's debt crisis. *World Policy Journal* 7(4), pp. 733–71.

Fishbein, J. A. and Woodall, P. (2006a). *Subprime Locations: Patterns of Geographic Disparity in Subprime Lending.* Washington, DC: Consumer Federation of America.

Fishbein, J. A. and Woodall, P. (2006b). *Women Are Prime Targets for Subprime Lending: Women Are Disproportionately Represented in High-Cost Mortgage Market.* Washington, DC: Consumer Federation of America.

General Accountability Office. (2009). *Troubled Asset Relief Program: Status of Efforts to Address Transparency and Accountability Issues.* GAO-09-296. Washington, DC: General Accountability Office.

General Accountability Office. (2011). *Troubled Federal Reserve System: Opportunities Exist to Strengthen Policies and Processes for Managing Emergency Assistance.* GAO-11-696. Washington, DC: General Accountability Office.

Ghosh, J., Heintz, J., and Pollin, R. (2012). Speculation on commodity futures markets and destabilization of global food prices: exploring the connections. *International Journal of Health Services* 42(3), pp. 465–83.

Gorton, G. and Rouwenhorst, K. G. (2006). Facts and fantasies about commodity futures. *Financial Analysts Journal* 62(2), pp. 47–68.

International Monetary Fund. (2015). All Commodity Price Index, Monthly. Available at: http://www.imf.org/external/np/res/commod/index.aspx [Accessed 27 Nov. 2015].

Kahn, L. (2010). The long-term labor consequences of graduating from college in a bad economy. *Labour Economics* 17(2), pp. 303–16.

Mills, C. W. (1999). *The Racial Contract.* Ithaca, NY: Cornell University Press.

Minsky, H. (1986). *Stabilizing an Unstable Economy.* New Haven, CT: Yale University Press.

Ndikumana, L. and Boyce, J. (2011). *Africa's Odious Debts: How Foreign Loans and Capital Flight Bled a Continent.* London: Zed Books.

Pastor, M. (1989). Latin America: The Debt Crisis and the International Monetary Fund, *Latin American Perspectives* 16(1), pp. 79–109.

Reich, R. (2011). *Aftershock: The Next Economy and America's Future.* New York: Vintage.

Seguino, S. and Heintz, J. (2012). Contractionary monetary policy and the dynamics of U.S. race and gender stratification. *American Journal of Economics and Sociology* 71(3), pp. 603–38.

UNCTAD. (2009). *Trade and Development Report 2009*. New York and Geneva: United Nations Conference on Trade and Development.

UNCTAD. (2011). *Price Formation in Financialized Commodity Markets: The Role of Information*. New York and Geneva: United Nations Conference on Trade and Development.

United Nations High Commissioner for Refugees (UNHCR). (2010). *Submission by the United Nations High Commissioner for Refugees for the Office of the High Commissioner for Human Rights' Compilation Report, Universal Periodic Review: GREECE*. Geneva: UNHCR.

7   Extraterritorial obligations, human rights, and economic governance[1]

The economies of the world have become increasingly interconnected. What happens in one economy spills over to other economies. Financial flows and productive resources are mobile across national boundaries and shift in response to changing economic conditions. Business entities operate in many countries simultaneously and move operations and activities between their affiliates. Production processes are fragmented and organized into global supply chains, with different stages of production occurring across a range of countries. The growing integration of the world's economies means that actions taken by one government affect the economic environment elsewhere. Moreover, the liberalization of financial flows between countries limits the policies governments are able to adopt. These changes pose fundamental challenges to the ability of governments to fulfill their obligations to support the realization of human rights (Coomans 2011).

In the previous chapter we explained how economies have become interconnected and interdependent, using the 2008 financial crisis as a salient example of the implications for this. In this chapter, we examine these relationships and their implications for the fulfillment of economic and social rights. Extraterritorial obligations refer to acts and omissions of a government that affect the enjoyment of rights outside of the state's own territory (Maastricht Principles 2012).[2] Given the current process of globalization, the question of extraterritorial obligations is central to understanding the barriers to realizing human rights. Extraterritorial obligations are relevant for a range of economic issues—from the behavior of transnational corporations to trade and investment policies. In this chapter, we focus on the role of businesses, those that operate across international borders, and monetary and financial policies, areas in which the connections between a state's extraterritorial obligations and the realization of rights are just beginning to be explored.

We begin by examining the definition and scope of extraterritorial obligations, with emphasis on the interpretation of extraterritorial obligations developed in the Maastricht Principles on Extraterritorial Obligations of States in the Area of Economic, Social and Cultural Rights (2012), and consider how these concepts apply to transnational corporations, monetary policy and the policy space available to governments. The chapter then turns to the issues of financial globalization and the extraterritorial aspects of the obligation to protect. We argue that an effective policy response requires international coordination across countries and briefly consider the implications for global institutions. This may require rethinking existing institutions such as the World Bank, the IMF, and the G20, and creating new institutions that would allow for greater international cooperation with regard to economic policy.

Extraterritorial obligations and the Maastricht Principles

The International Covenant on Economic, Social and Cultural Rights (ICESCR 1966) recognizes that a country has obligations with regard to the realization of economic and social rights beyond its borders.[3] Specifically, as discussed in other chapters, Article 2, para 1 of the ICESCR states that states should

> take steps, individually and through international assistance and cooperation, especially economic and technical, to the maximum of its available resources, with a view to achieving progressively the full realization of the rights recognized in the present Covenant by all appropriate means.

Although the ICESCR recognizes the need for "international assistance and cooperation" it does not provide a framework for interpreting the scope, application, and nature of this obligation. Specifically, the ICESCR does not provide sufficient guidance on critical aspects of international law, such as state sovereignty and jurisdiction (Skogly and Gibney 2010). Often, "international assistance" is interpreted as an obligation of high-income countries to provide financial and other resources to poorer countries, e.g. obligation with regard to official development assistance (ODA)—an issue discussed in Chapter 5 (Künnemann 2004). International law implies a commitment to international cooperation, yet the nature and extent of this cooperation with regard to economic and social rights has not been clearly spelled out in international agreements (Coomans and Kamminga 2004).

The potential scope of international cooperation and assistance has been explored for a variety of areas: international sanctions, official development assistance, international trade, and corporate conduct. With regard to global institutions and governance, the obligations of states as members of influential international organizations that can shape the policies adopted by governments, such as the International Monetary Fund and the World Bank, have received significant attention (Salomon 2007; Coomans and Kamminga 2004). One area that has received less attention is how the implementation of economic policy, including financial policies and regulations, by one country affects the policy choices available elsewhere in ways which have implications for the realization of economic and social rights (Salomon 2007).

Treaty bodies have elaborated extraterritorial obligations with regard to human rights numerous times.[4] For instance, the Committee on Economic, Social and Cultural Rights has further interpreted aspects of the international obligations with regard to economic and social rights (Sepúlveda 2006). General Comment 12 of the Committee focuses on the right to food and explicitly emphasizes international support, cooperation and obligations in the realization of the right to food (Künnemann 2004). Similarly, in the General Comment on the Right to Health the Committee recognizes a collective responsibility to confront the health risks associated with diseases that can be transmitted across international borders, including the ability of low-income countries to meet these challenges (Coomans 2011). Although the General Comment is focused on health, there are important parallels to other areas. The need to confront issues of contagion through international cooperation has direct parallels with critical economic issues, such as the spread of financial crises from one country to another.

The ability to hold governments to account for their obligations with regard to international cooperation and assistance depends on the existence of institutional and governance mechanisms to facilitate this process. For instance, the Committee has put in place an Optional Protocol to the ICESCR to provide a complaint mechanism. In the deliberations leading up to the Optional Protocol, the question of how and whether international cooperation should be incorporated had been controversial (Sepúlveda 2006). The design of these kinds of institutional arrangements will have significant implications for the scope and interpretation of extraterritorial obligations to facilitate the realization of economic and social rights. They also affect governance issues associated with the fundamental crosscutting principles which underpin the ICESCR, such as accountability, transparency, and participation (Ibid.). These principles are critical for ensuring that civil society has the ability to hold states to account for their extraterritorial obligations. With regard to the specific topic of this chapter, global institutions are critical for the coordination of economic, financial and regulatory policies that have cross-border effects, an issue we return to later.

As discussed, the ICESCR lacked a detailed framework for defining the scope and nature of extraterritorial obligations. Given this gap, in 2011, a group of experts on international law and human rights convened in Maastricht in order to develop and elaborate a core set of principles on extraterritorial obligations in the area of economic, social, and cultural rights. The result was the Maastricht Principles on Extraterritorial Obligations of States in the Area of Economic, Social and Cultural Rights that explicitly recognized that the policies adopted by governments affect the realization of rights beyond their own borders. The preamble to the Maastricht Principles states:

> The human rights of individuals, groups, and peoples are affected by and dependent on the extraterritorial acts and omissions of States. The advent of economic globalization in particular, has meant that States and other global actors exert considerable influence on the realization of economic, social, and cultural rights across the world.

The Maastricht Principles reaffirmed the existing framework for economic, social, and cultural rights, as developed in the Universal Declaration of Human Rights, the International Covenant on Economic, Social and Cultural Rights, and other international agreements. However, they further elaborated the concept of extraterritorial obligations with regard to jurisdiction, responsibilities, and existing human rights obligations, including the obligations to respect, protect, and fulfill.[5] Therefore, the Maastricht Principles have far-reaching implications for the formulation and conduct of economic policies, the creation of an appropriate regulatory framework, the practices of international organizations, and limits on the behavior of transnational businesses.

A primary aim of the Principles is to shed light on and clarify the legal parameters in which obligations with respect to social and economic rights are discharged (Salomon and Seiderman 2012). These Principles were signed on to by a group of experts and are based on existing international law.[6] The Maastricht Principles have been further supported by expert commentary that identifies the existing treaties, agreements, and covenants which provide a legal foundation for the Principles (De Schutter et al. 2012). It is important to note that the Maastricht Principles are not, at the current time, legally binding on governments, but represent an authoritative interpretation of the extraterritorial human rights obligations of states.[7] In this regard, it represents an important step towards assessing the implications of global economic interdependencies on the realization of economic and social rights. One of the central issues associated with extraterritorial obligations is the question of jurisdiction: whether human rights agreements extend to situations outside of the state's territory (Salomon and Seiderman 2012; De Schutter et al. 2012; Skogly and Gibney 2010). An essential contribution of the Maastricht Principles is to clarify when jurisdiction for human rights obligations applies beyond territorial borders.

Obligations with regard to economic and social rights are often discussed with regard to the threefold typology: the obligation to respect rights, the obligation to fulfill rights and the obligation to protect rights (Coomans and Kamminga 2004; Sepúlveda 2006). This same typology can be applied to international cooperation, and the Maastricht Principles provide guidelines for thinking about each of these obligations and how they apply to the question of extraterritorial obligations (Principles 19–35). It is helpful to summarize these guidelines here.[8]

With regard to the obligation to respect rights, the Maastricht Principles recognize two ways in which the state may interfere with the enjoyment of economic and social rights outside of the state's territory: direct interference and indirect interference (Maastricht Principles 2012, Principles 20 and 21). Direct interference refers to conduct by the state itself that impairs the realization of economic and social rights of people outside their territories. In contrast, indirect interference refers to actions by one state which undermine the ability of another state or international organization to comply with economic and social rights obligations. This can happen, for instance, if the policy choices of one government determine the policy space available to another government in ways that undermine the realization of rights. As we will see, indirect interference with the obligation to respect rights may represent a significant impediment to the enjoyment of economic and social rights.

With regard to macroeconomic governance, the obligations to fulfill and protect economic and social rights are particularly important. The extraterritorial dimensions of the obligation to fulfill rights, as spelled out in the Maastricht Principles, include the requirement that states should create an environment conducive to realizing rights through their own policy choices and through international cooperation in a range of different areas: international trade, investment, finance, taxation, environmental protection, and development cooperation (Maastricht Principles 2012, Principle 29). Engaging in meaningful international coordination is central to the extraterritorial aspects of the obligation to fulfill. This includes actions within international organizations—such as the United Nations, UN agencies, the World Bank, the International Monetary Fund, and the World Trade Organization among others—that contribute to the fulfillment of economic and social rights within and beyond each state's own territory.

The extraterritorial aspects of the obligation to protect are also enumerated within the Maastricht Principles, with significant implications for economic policy, financial governance, and policing the actions of businesses operating across national boundaries (Maastricht Principles 2012, Principles 23–27). The obligation to protect includes the obligation to establish a regulatory environment that prevents international organizations, transnational corporations, and individuals from taking actions that undermine the realization of rights beyond a state's borders (De Schutter et al. 2012). These extraterritorial obligations include omissions by the state, such as one state's failure to adequately regulate the actions of third parties in a way that has negative consequences for rights elsewhere (Maastricht Principles 2012, Principle 24).

Transnational corporations and businesses

Businesses are important social institutions and their behavior directly affects the realization of rights. Increasingly, businesses organize their economic activities across international borders, and this raises questions about the extraterritorial obligations of governments to regulate businesses that operate in other countries in ways consistent with the full range of human rights obligations. With regard to business activities that threaten rights, the Maastricht Principles hold that governments must enforce measures to protect economic and social rights beyond their borders when the company concerned is either registered, has its main place of business, or has its center of activity in that country concerned (Maastricht Principles 2012, Principle 24). This applies to all kinds of businesses—both financial and non-financial—and has implications for a broad range of issues, from labor standards at work to the policy space available to governments.

Human rights experts have engaged with the question of the relationship between business and human rights, although the framework continues to evolve. In 2005 the Human Rights Council requested that the Secretary-General appoint a Special Representative to look at human rights, transnational corporations and other types of business enterprises.[9] The Special Representative was charged with identifying businesses' responsibilities with regard to human rights; clarifying the role of the state in regulating businesses and developing an approach to performing human rights impact assessments of the activities of corporations and other businesses. In 2011, a set of Guiding Principles on Business and Human Rights, developed by Special Representative John Ruggie (the "Ruggie Principles"), were endorsed by the Human Rights Council.

The Guiding Principles on Business and Human Rights state that "Business enterprises should respect human rights. This means that they should avoid infringing on the human rights of others and should address adverse human rights impacts with which they are involved" (OHCHR 2011, Principle 11). However, the Guiding Principles are less definitive when it comes to the question of extraterritorial obligations and the role of the state with respect to business activities outside its territory:

> At present States are not generally required under international human rights law to regulate the extraterritorial activities of businesses domiciled in their territory and/or jurisdiction. Nor are they generally prohibited from doing so, provided there is a recognized jurisdictional basis. Within these parameters some human rights treaty bodies recommend that home States take steps to prevent abuse abroad by business enterprises within their jurisdiction.
>
> (Ibid., Principle 2)

This ambiguity exists because, at the current time, there is no definitive framework within human rights treaties and agreements that governs the behavior of transnational corporations.

Nevertheless, mandate holders for UN Special Procedures have communicated with governments on the issue of extraterritorial obligations, particularly in cases involving abuse of human rights by businesses operating in another country. For example, in 2013, acting on information that a South Korean steel factory in India could threaten to displace over 20,000 people from their homes and land, eight UN mandate holders wrote to the Republic of Korea stressing the importance of recognizing the country's extraterritorial obligations (ESCR-Net 2014).

In an effort to begin to address this gap in international human rights law, in 2014, the Human Rights Council established an Intergovernmental Working Group (IGWG) on transnational corporations and human rights. The mandate of the IGWG is to "elaborate an international legally binding instrument to regulate, in international human rights law, the activities of transnational corporations and other business enterprises" (OHCHR 2014). The first session of the IGWG was held in July 2015.[10] The program of work focused on defining states' human rights obligations with respect to transnational corporations and the ways in which transnational corporations are currently governed in international law.

These developments demonstrate that increasing attention is being paid to the activities of transnational corporations, the extraterritorial obligations of states with regard to business, and the implications of greater global integration for the realization of rights. At the current time, this framework is evolving, but remains critical for developing strategies for the full realization of human rights and designing the institutions of global governance needed to make it happen.

Monetary policy, capital flows, and extraterritorial obligations

The extraterritorial obligations of states with regard to economic governance are not limited to the regulation of business activities. There are also far-reaching issues associated with the policy choices governments make. We begin with a consideration of monetary policy as an area of macroeconomic governance in which extraterritorial obligations are relevant. Actions by one country in the conduct of monetary policy, particularly a large influential economy, can affect the macroeconomic environment of other countries in ways that potentially undermine the realization of economic and social rights. As Mary Dowell-Jones (2012) points out, "Problems that emerge in esoteric financial markets like credit derivatives can rapidly contaminate broader financial markets and the global economy, causing huge human costs." In addition, policy choices by one state can have an impact on interest rates, exchange rates and capital flows elsewhere. Moreover, these decisions affect the policy space of other countries, limiting the choices available to support economic and social rights.

To give a concrete example, suppose the central bank of a large influential country—e.g. the Federal Reserve in the United States—decides to raise interest rates. It may raise rates because of a policy target to keep inflation at very low levels. Higher interest rates make credit more expensive and tend to lower spending on consumption and investment. Lower levels of spending reduce pressures on prices in the economy and, through this channel, can lower inflation. However, increases in interest rates in an influential economy can affect interest rates beyond its borders. Specifically, other countries will suddenly face pressures to also raise their interest rates. This occurs because investors tend to move financial resources out of low interest rate economies and into higher interest rate economies.

To prevent these kinds of outflows, countries may have to take steps to raise rates in response to a policy move elsewhere. Raising interest rates potentially limits the level of borrowing in the country and can slow down the economy. Therefore an increase in interest rates in the US has the potential to decrease borrowing in another country that is trying to stop capital outflows. Higher interest rates and slower growth affect the realization of economic and social rights through a number of channels. Slower growth limits the resources available to realize rights—including resources to support government spending. Higher interest rates make borrowing—both public and private—more expensive. As we discuss below, this limits a government's ability to respond to a crisis by borrowing to support state expenditures during a downturn. Similarly, higher interest rates can also affect specific rights—such as the right to housing— by affecting the costs of mortgage payments and the risk of default and foreclosure.

Similar dynamics are involved with exchange rates. If an influential economy devalues its exchange rate—i.e. makes its currency less expensive relative to other currencies—the goods and services it exports will become relatively cheaper, while imports will become more expensive. Other countries may find that the volume of goods and services they are able to sell abroad drops off, and imported products become more attractive than those produced domestically. In order to counteract these trends, states may respond by lowering their own exchange rates. Once again, policy choices taken in one country affect key macroeconomic variables and the policy choices adopted elsewhere.

How do these macroeconomic dynamics affect the realization of economic and social rights? As described earlier, higher interest rates reduce consumption and investment in ways that slow economic activity. The outcome may be a loss of employment opportunities and higher rates of unemployment or underemployment, with a direct bearing on the right to work and an adequate standard of living. Studies have found that, in some countries, restrictive monetary policies affect women's employment more than men's, raising issues of non-discrimination and equality (Braunstein and Heintz 2008). Interest rate policy likely contributed to the subprime mortgage crisis in the United States. The Federal Reserve raised its policy interest rate prior to the crisis, contributing to the upward pressures on the monthly payments for adjustable rate mortgages (Heintz and Balakrishnan 2012). The foreclosures that resulted from the subprime crisis undermined the right to housing.

Similarly, shifts in exchange rates affect the realization of rights. A devalued exchange rate raises the costs of imported products relative to exports. For some countries—e.g. those that rely on imported essentials—a devaluation could mean a higher price for food or other basic goods. This lowers living standards and threatens access to food, outcomes with important consequences for the realization of economic and social rights. The relationship between these macroeconomic variables and human rights outcomes will vary across countries, but the more general point is that these dynamics have potentially important consequences for economic and social rights.

The interactions between interest rate and exchange rate policies in different countries are linked to a concept of an economic "trilemma".[11] The trilemma states that three conditions cannot hold simultaneously: (1) having a fixed exchange rate; (2) conducting independent monetary policy; and (3) allowing the free movement of capital (i.e. free financial flows between countries). If financial capital is free to move between economies, a country can use policies to influence exchange rates or interest rates, but not both. For instance, if a country lowers interest rates through monetary policy, financial outflows to the rest of the world will increase, causing an exchange rate devaluation. On the other hand, if a country tries to prevent such a devaluation, it must raise interest rates (or cannot lower them) in order to reduce financial outflows. Higher interest rates or a devaluation of the currency affect the realization of economic and social rights through the channels already discussed.

Policy choices and real outcomes in different countries are connected through similar dynamics involving inflows and outflows of financial capital. Empirical studies have uncovered evidence of these linkages. Foreign interest rates have been shown to have a negative impact on growth in high-income developed economies, with this relationship being sensitive to exchange rate policies (di Giovanni and Shambaugh 2007). In other words, interest rates in one country can affect real economic performance elsewhere, and, as discussed, affect the realization of economic and social rights. This raises important issues of extraterritorial obligations with respect to the conduct of monetary policy.

These issues are relevant to the extraterritorial dimensions of the obligation to fulfill, as described in the Maastricht Principles. The Principles stress the need to create an "enabling environment" for the realization of rights, both domestically and extraterritorially, as part of a state's obligation to fulfill economic and social rights (2012, Principle 20). Applied to monetary policy would suggest that those conducting interest rate and exchange rate policy in one country should consider the effects that it has on the macroeconomic environment elsewhere. Pushed further, the ICESCR's language on international cooperation and the Maastricht Principles' discussion of the obligation to fulfill would imply that policy choices should be coordinated across countries in ways that facilitate the enjoyment of economic and social rights. We will return to this issue of global cooperation and macroeconomic governance later in the chapter.

Financial globalization, contagion, and crisis

The 2008 financial crisis demonstrated how macroeconomic and financial dynamics affect the environment for realizing economic and social rights on a global scale.[12] The crisis was associated with dramatic declines in production and trade, rapidly rising unemployment, plunging government revenues, foreclosures, growing indebtedness, and a dramatic loss of wealth.[13] The crisis had devastating effects with regard to a range of economic and social rights: the right to work, the right to housing, the right to food, the right to education, and the right to an adequate standard of living. Moreover, the policy response in many countries—the adoption of austerity programs to reduce indebtedness primarily through cuts in government spending—creates further challenges for the realization of human rights obligations, an issue addressed in Chapter 8. Because of the global nature of the crisis and because the crisis was due, at least in part, to government policies and government omissions in terms of taking proactive steps to prevent the crisis, extraterritorial obligations are relevant to the issues of financial globalization and economic fragility.[14]

We define financial globalization to refer to the greater integration of financial markets across international borders, the expansion of the operations of financial institutions into new markets in other economies, increases in international acquisitions of banks and other financial institutions, and the growing tendency of investors to acquire securities and financial products from a range of countries beyond the country in which they are based (Epstein 2005). The 2008 financial crisis provides a compelling example of how financial globalization creates pathways of contagion through which economic crises can be transmitted across borders. More generally, financial globalization creates the conditions for the extraterritorial transmission of a variety of economic shocks, both real and monetary (Goldberg 2009).

For instance, research that examined the channels through which US GDP shocks are transmitted across industrialized countries found that the macroeconomic variables with the largest spillover effects are financial in character—e.g. interest rates, bond yields, and stock prices (Bayoumi and

Swiston 2007). Similarly, financial channels appear to play an important role in transmitting shocks in the US economy to countries in Latin America (Canova 2005). Therefore, the process of financial globalization makes the issue of extraterritorial obligations with respect to the conduct of economic policy more pressing. Actions or omissions by one country that negatively impact its own economy and financial markets can be quickly passed on to other economies, with financial pathways playing a prominent role in the economic epidemiology of crises and contagion (Jones 2012).

Financial globalization also alters the effectiveness of monetary policy and the channels through which monetary policy operates. The lending channel is one of the ways in which contractionary monetary policy (i.e. raising interest rates or reducing credit supply) is assumed to affect economic activity and price levels—i.e. altering the cost and availability of credit through its impact on the ability of banks to access funds.[15] Therefore, the effectiveness of monetary policy would be weakened if banks have access to alternative sources of funds when the central bank pursues a contractionary policy (Cetorelli and Goldberg 2008). Banks with global operations may respond to tighter monetary policy by drawing on overseas sources of liquidity within their internal networks (Ibid.).

Economists working at the Federal Reserve Bank of New York present evidence that this is indeed the case for US banks—more globalized banks limit the effectiveness of domestic monetary policy (Cetorelli and Goldberg 2008). Moreover, global banks tend to be larger institutions and restrictive monetary policy appears to have a larger impact on the credit extended by smaller, domestic banking institutions.[16] This suggests that the trend toward more consolidated, increasingly globalized banks in economies like the US has important implications for the conduct of monetary policy. The study also finds that contractionary monetary policy has an effect on the cost of credit of global banks operating offices in *other* countries—i.e. financial globalization creates channels through which monetary policy affects credit conditions elsewhere, but limits its effectiveness domestically (Ibid.). We have argued that the policy space available to governments to adopt their own discretionary monetary and financial sector policies has important implications for the obligations to fulfill and protect. Therefore, the dynamics of financial globalization raise important questions regarding extraterritoriality and macroeconomic policy choices.

Recent economic crises also raise important concerns about the extraterritorial dimensions of the obligation to protect. Changes in regulatory regimes involving financial markets and financial flows has been linked to recent economic crises. For instance, the liberalization of the movement of finance capital between countries appears to have contributed to the global financial crisis of 1997, which had a large impact on East Asian economies (Stiglitz 2000). Similarly, the rollback of regulatory controls on US banks and financial institutions has been identified as a structural change contributing to the 2008 meltdown in US financial markets and the subsequent global financial crisis (Stiglitz 2008).[17] In other words, economic crises are not episodes of misfortune that are unconnected with governments, their policy choices, and any failure to maintain an adequate regulatory framework. The actions of third parties—e.g. financial corporations and global investors engaged in speculative activities—are the proximate causes of such crises. Therefore, the failure to regulate financial markets in ways that reduce or minimize the likelihood of economic crises represents a failure of the obligation to protect with significant extraterritorial dimensions.

The structure of international finance not only affects the dynamics leading to economic fragility and the channels through which crises are transmitted from one country to the next. It also impacts policy responses. Larger, more systemically influential economies have a wider range of policy options available when responding to economic shocks compared to smaller, more dependent economies and those that occupy more peripheral positions in the global economy (Ocampo 2010). Some economies, such as the US and China, were able to respond to the 2008 crisis by implementing counter-cyclical stimulus policies in an effort to at least partially offset the negative consequences of the financial shock (ILO 2011). However, a similar economic shock may have different effects on less well-positioned economies, which may experience capital outflows as financial investors seek out safe havens (Ocampo 2010). Under these conditions, more vulnerable economies tend to implement pro-cyclical policies such as higher interest rates and cuts to government spending in an effort to stem financial outflows (Ocampo and Vos 2008). The result is unbalanced policy responses to a global crisis with distinct consequences for economic and social rights. Countries that are able to implement economic stimulus policies can take steps to mitigate any backsliding due to the crisis, but many other countries will adopt policy positions which could contribute to, rather than alleviate, retrogression with regard to social and economic rights—e.g. raising interest rates or adopting austerity programs that cut government social spending.

These asymmetries in the policy responses to economic crises are not pre-ordained, but rather are a result of the structure of the global economy and the ways in which capital flows between countries are managed. A coordinated policy response—one that tries to preserve the policy space available to countries in more vulnerable positions—would create the possibility for alternatives to a pro-cyclical response in the wake of an economic crisis. Global macroeconomic governance is critical here. International institutions could play a coordinating role so that countries experiencing capital outflows are not disproportionately affected by a global shock. However, institutions such as the International Monetary Fund typically impose conditionalities on their emergency lending that reinforce existing asymmetries in global macroeconomic governance.[18] If extraterritorial obligations, as outlined in the Maastricht Principles, are to be taken seriously, there is a real need to transform the existing system of global economic governance to allow more coordinated responses.

Extraterritorial obligations, global institutions, and international cooperation

The economic interdependence of nations affects the formulation of macroeconomic and financial policies to support the enjoyment of economic and social rights. Under these conditions, a single country acting alone may not have sufficient latitude for formulating and implementing economic policies which foster an environment for the progressive realization of these rights. Under these circumstances, global cooperation is necessary for the effective management of these interdependencies. As discussed previously, Article 2(1) of the ICESCR stresses the need for international cooperation for the realization of economic and social rights. Moreover, Principle 30 of the Maastricht Principles says that "States should coordinate with each other ... in order to cooperate effectively in the universal fulfilment of economic, social and cultural rights. The lack of such coordination does not exonerate a State from giving effect to its separate extraterritorial obligations" (2012).

Uncoordinated approaches to macroeconomic management not only restrict policy space, but also may result in the inefficient use of resources.[19] For instance, some countries have accumulated large stocks of foreign exchange reserves as an insurance policy against future economic crises. These resources cannot be pressed into service to support the realization of rights and therefore represent a cost of uncoordinated policies (this issue was also discussed in Chapter 5). Furthermore, an uncoordinated approach to financial regulation will prove to be ineffective. Financial investors can avoid an oasis of regulation in a select number of countries by circumventing these markets. Regulations in key financial centers may be more critical than regulations elsewhere. For instance, the most influential commodity futures markets are concentrated in a few locations: New York, Chicago, and London. How these major markets are regulated has implications for commodity price dynamics. Therefore, a common approach to global financial governance, requiring effective global institutions, is essential.

The need for such coordination is explicitly recognized in the Maastricht Principles (2012, Principle 30). Concerns over a failure of global economic governance reached new heights in the aftermath of the 2008 crisis. Since the 1980s, the trend has been towards liberalizing markets, yet unrestricted financial markets engender financial fragility, heighten volatility, and create the propensity for crises, as the experience of the past several decades has shown (Stiglitz 2000). Influential international players recognized that the global institutions to support a coordinated approach to managing finance were insufficient and this was the rationale for elevating the role of the G20 in coordinating macroeconomic policy (Heintz 2013). Despite its elevated role, the G20's effectiveness in implementing a coordinated approach to financial regulation remains inadequate (Ibid.).

According to the Maastricht Principles "A State that transfers competences to, or participates in, an international organization must take all reasonable steps to ensure that the relevant organization acts consistently with the international human rights obligations of that State" (2012, Principle 15). The ETO principles have implications for the ways in which institutions such as the IMF, the WTO and the World Bank could be held accountable to a set of human rights obligations, if the extraterritorial obligations laid out in the Maastricht Principles, for example, were legally binding and enforced. The implications of the call for international cooperation for the realization of economic and social rights has been recognized in arguments developed in greater detail elsewhere (Salomon 2007). In addition, as has already been discussed, the current system for managing international financial flows also reinforces existing inequities between countries. Developing countries often have access to global finance on unequal terms, since their integration into global markets is segmented by perceptions of risk and creditworthiness. This creates conditions under which financial volatility has larger impacts on the economies of developing nations compared to high-income countries (Ocampo 2010).

Financial stability, a strong regulatory environment and appropriate macroeconomic management for the realization of rights have the character of a "global public good." Global public goods refer to goods and services whose benefits transcend national borders.[20] Coordination to ensure that there is an adequate supply of global public goods represents a particularly critical challenge since the provision of such goods and services has traditionally been seen to be the role of national governments, yet nation states, acting independently, cannot guarantee that global public goods will be adequately supplied—since such regulations are costly to individual governments and the benefits spill over national borders. When public goods have a global character, there is often an absence of institutions capable of overcoming the coordination failures associated with the provision of public goods. Existing institutions are often hampered by coordination failures between states—i.e. when countries protect their national interest instead of pursuing a coordinated approach. The failure to date to reach a comprehensive agreement on reductions in greenhouse gas emissions endorsed by all countries provides an example of these dynamics—i.e. individual countries prefer to opt out of such agreements to avoid the costs of adjustment associated with reducing pollutants that are harmful at the global level.

There is a need to consider global institutions which are capable of creating a system of economic governance which supports, not undermines, human rights. This raises important questions about whether the extraterritorial obligations, as laid out in the Maastricht Principles, are sufficient for achieving this kind of global cooperation. If all states adhere to these extraterritorial obligations, taking into account the external effects of their actions on others, the result would be the kind of coordination necessary for supporting economic and social rights globally. However, in the absence of the universal application of these principles, extraterritorial obligations will fall short of true multilateral global cooperation. We can imagine a situation in which one state supports its extraterritorial obligations while other governments choose to opt out. When reciprocity in honoring extraterritorial obligations across all states is imperfect and incomplete, the outcomes will fall short of what could be achieved under true international coordination.

The Maastricht Principles outline some mechanisms for ensuring compliance with a state's extraterritorial obligations, including the need for accountability, a requirement for states to provide effective remedies for the violation of rights, and the need for interstate complaint mechanisms (2012, Principles 36, 39). With regard to international coordination, the interstate complaint mechanisms are particularly important. However, the focus remains on existing human rights agreements, treaties, international institutions and institutions to ensure this kind of cooperation, often without a clear means of sanctioning states for non-compliance or providing the appropriate institutional support for global cooperation. Because of this, the question of what types of global institutions need to be put in place to support a more universal application of these extraterritorial obligations remains an open one.

Conclusion

Although it has been long recognized that states have extraterritorial obligations that bear on the realization of economic and social rights, the nature of these obligations has not been fully developed or expounded upon in detail. The Maastricht Principles represent an important first step in providing a more detailed interpretation of these extraterritorial obligations—including the obligation to regulate businesses whose activities span international borders. Financial globalization has affected the policy space available to governments operating independently in liberalized market economies. It has created channels through which actions and omissions of states affect the realization of rights across international boundaries, with financial channels playing an increasingly dominant role. All of these developments carry with them critical implications for extraterritorial obligations relating to economic and social rights.

This chapter has argued that international coordination is essential for supporting individual states' ability to meet the obligations to protect, respect, and fulfill rights. Such global cooperation could be achieved through the universal acceptance of extraterritorial obligations. In the absence of the universal application of these principles, important questions surface concerning the best way to conduct economic policies to realize economic and social rights in a context of global integration. The solution will lie with the creation of institutions to support policy coordination across countries. The current set of global institutions does not appear up to the task, which raises important issues of how to move forward in the future to create a global economy that supports, rather than undermines, core human rights.

Notes

1   Portions of this chapter incorporate material from a previously published book chapter. Radhika Balakrishnan and James Heintz. (2014). Extraterritorial obligations, financial globalization, and macroeconomic governance. In A. Nolan, ed. *Economic and Social Rights after the Global Financial Crisis*. Cambridge, UK: Cambridge University Press, pp. 146–66. © 2014 Cambridge University Press. Reprinted with permission.

2   Extraterritorial obligations should not be confused with the doctrine of humanitarian intervention that has used human rights to try to justify military interventions in other countries.

3   See, for example, Sepúlveda (2006); Coomans (2011); and Coomans and Kamminga, eds. (2004).

4   UN treaty bodies have considered the ETOs of states with regards to various rights, including the right to social security, the right to food, the right to not be tortured or ill-treated, the rights to water and housing, and the right to a remedy and reparation. See ESCR-Net (2014).

5   With regard to the obligations to respect, protect, and fulfill, see Maastricht Principles on Extraterritorial Obligations (2012): Principles 19–35.

6   For additional discussion of the relationship between extraterritorial obligations, the United Nations and international law, see The Global Initiative for Economic, Social and Cultural Rights (2015). www.etoconsortium.org/nc/en/library/documents/?tx_drblob_pi1%5BdownloadUid%5D=132.

7   These obligations are only legally binding on states that have ratified the legal instruments on which the Maastricht Principles are based.

8   See also, Center for Economic, Social, and Cultural Rights (2015).

9   The mandate of the Special Representative expired in 2011.

10   The first session consisted of panels of experts to clarify the issues and the existing framework for governing transnational corporations with regards to human rights and international law. Draft report available at: www.ohchr.org/EN/HRBodies/HRC/WGTransCorp/Session1/Pages/Draftreport.aspx [Accessed 19 Sept. 2015].

11   The concept of a trilemma can be traced to papers by Robert Mundell and Robert Fleming that form the basis of what is often called the "Mundell-Fleming Model". The trilemma is derived from this theoretical framework (Mundell 1962).

12   In this chapter, we date the beginning of the financial crisis to 2008, the year that, in US financial markets, Lehman Brothers went bankrupt and Bear Stearns, facing collapse, was absorbed by JP Morgan Chase through a government assisted acquisition. In 2008, the true global extent of the crisis

became evident. Some prefer 2007 as marking the beginning of the crisis, in part because this was the start of recession in the US economy. However, in 2007 the magnitude of the crisis with regard to the global economy still was not fully realized.

13 See, for example, Swagel (2009) and European Commission (2009). For an analytical overview of these and related issues in the context of economic and social rights, see Heintz and Balakrishnan (2012).

14 For in-depth analysis of how regulatory failures in the US contributed to the global economic crisis, see Financial Crisis Inquiry Commission (2011).

15 Specifically, contractionary monetary policy makes it more difficult or more expensive for banks to access resources for reservable deposits. When banks find it more difficult to maintain the reserves needed to support their current level of lending, they may cut back on the amount of credit they extend.

16 In this research study, global banks are defined as US banks that report positive assets from offices operating in other countries.

17 This will be discussed in detail in Chapter 8.

18 For a discussion of conditionalities imposed by international financial institutions as they relate to global cooperation and economic and social rights, see Salomon (2007).

19 This relates to the principle of the use of maximum available resources, put forward in Article 2(1) of the International Covenant on Economic, Social and Cultural Rights (1966).

20 See Kaul, Conceição, Goulven, and Mendoza, eds. (2003). Ocampo broadens the definition of global public goods to include all issues that belong in the public domain or are of public interest, see Ocampo (2010).

References

Balakrishnan, R. and Heintz, J. (2014) Extraterritorial obligations: Financial globalization and macroeconomic governance. In A. Nolan, ed., *Economic and Social Rights after the Global Financial Crisis*. Cambridge: Cambridge University Press, pp. 146–66.

Bayoumi, T. and Swiston, A. (2007). *Foreign Entanglements: Estimating the Source and Size of Spillovers across Industrial Countries*. IMF Working Paper WP/07/182. Washington DC: International Monetary Fund.

Braunstein, E. and Heintz, J. (2008). Gender bias and central bank policy: Employment and inflation reduction. *International Journal of Applied Economics* 22, pp. 173–86.

Canova, F. (2005). The transmission of US shocks to Latin America. *Journal of Applied Econometrics* 20, pp. 229–51.

Center for Economic and Social Rights (CESR). (2015). *Universal Rights, Differentiated Responsibilities: Safeguarding Human Rights beyond Borders to Achieve the Sustainable Development Goals. Human Rights Policy Briefing*. New York: CESR.

Cetorelli, N. and Goldberg, L. S. (2008). *Banking Globalization, Monetary Transmission, and the Lending Channel*. NBER Working Paper 14101. Cambridge, MA: National Bureau of Economic Research.

Coomans, F. (2011). The extraterritorial scope of the International Covenant on Economic, Social and Cultural Rights in the work of the United Nations Committee on Economic, Social, and Cultural Rights. *Human Rights Law Review* 11(1), pp. 1–35.

Coomans, F. and Kamminga, M. T., eds. (2004). *Extraterritorial Application of Human Rights Treaties*. Antwerp-Oxford: Intersentia.

De Schutter, O., Eide, A., Kalfan, A., Orellana, M., Salomon, M., and Seiderman, I. (2012). Commentary to the Maastricht Principles on Extraterritorial Obligations of States in the Area of Economic, Social, and Cultural Rights. *Human Rights Quarterly* 34, pp. 1084–1169.

di Giovanni, J. and Shambaugh, J. (2007). *The Impact of Foreign Interest Rates on the Economy: The Role of the Exchange Rate Regime*. Paper. Hanover, NH: Dartmouth College.

Dowell-Jones, M.J. (2012). International finance and human rights: Scope for a mutually beneficial relationship. *Global Policy* 3, pp. 467–70.

Epstein, G. (2005). Introduction: Financialization and the world economy. In: G. Epstein, ed., *Financialization and the World Economy*. Northampton, MA: Edward Elgar, pp. 3–16.

ESCR-Net. (2014). *Global Economy, Global Rights: A Practitioners' Guide for Interpreting Human Rights Obligations in the Global Economy*. New York: ESCR-Net.

European Commission. (2009). *Economic Crisis in Europe: Causes, Consequences, and Responses*. European Economy No. 7. Luxembourg: Office for Official Publications of the European Communities.

Financial Crisis Inquiry Commission. (2011). *The Financial Crisis Inquiry Report*. Washington, DC: The Financial Crisis Inquiry Commission Pursuant to Public Law 111-21.

The Global Initiative for Economic, Social and Cultural Rights. (2015). *Human Rights Law Sources: UN Pronouncements and International Law*. Working Paper. Geneva. Available at: www.etoconsortium.org/nc/en/library/documents/?tx_drblob_pi1%5BdownloadUid%5D=132.

Goldberg, L.S. (2009). Understanding banking sector globalization. *IMF Staff Papers* 56, pp. 171–97.

Heintz, J. (2013). *Missing Women: The G-20, Gender Equality and Global Economic Governance*. Berlin: Heinrich Böll Foundation.

Heintz, J. and Balakrishnan, R. (2012). Debt, power, and crisis: Social stratification and the inequitable governance of financial markets. *American Quarterly* 64, pp. 387–409.

International Covenant on Economic, Social and Cultural Rights (ICESCR). (1966). Office of the High Commissioner for Human Rights. Available at: http://www.ohchr.org/EN/ProfessionalInterest/Pages/CESCR.aspx [Accessed 26 Sept. 2015].

International Labor Organization (ILO). (2011). *A Review of Global Stimulus*. EC-IILS Joint Discussion Paper Series No. 5. Geneva: ILO.

Jones, M.D. (2012). International finance and human rights: Scope for a mutually beneficial relationship. *Global Policy* 3, pp. 467–70.

Kaul, I., Conceição, P., Goulven, K., and Mendoza, R. U., eds. (2003). *Providing Global Public Goods: Managing Globalization*. New York: United Nations Development Program.

Künnemann, R. (2004). Extraterritorial application of the International Covenant on Economic, Social and Cultural Rights. In F. Coomans and M.T. Kamminga, eds., *Extraterritorial Application of Human Rights Treaties*. Antwerp-Oxford: Intersentia, pp. 201–31.

Maastricht Principles on Extraterritorial Obligations of States in the Area of Economic, Social and Cultural Rights. (2012). Available at: http://www. etoconsortium.org/nc/en/library/maastricht-principles/?tx_drblob_pi1[downloadUid]=23 [Accessed 27 Sept. 2015].

Mundell, R. (1962). Capital mobility and stabilization policy under fixed and flexible exchange rates. *Canadian Journal of Economic and Political Science* 29, pp. 475–85.

Ocampo, J. A. (2010). Rethinking global economic and social governance. *Journal of Globalization and Development*, Article 6.

Ocampo, J. A. and Vos, R. (2008). *Policy Space and the Changing Paradigm in Conducting Macroeconomic Policies in Developing Countries*. BIS Papers No. 36. Basel: Bank for International Settlement.

Office of the High Commissioner for Human Rights (OHCHR). (2011). *Guiding Principles on Business and Human Rights*. Geneva: OHCHR.

Office of the High Commissioner for Human Rights (OHCHR). (2014). *Elaboration of an International Legally Binding Instrument on Transnational Corporations and Other Business Enterprises with Respect to Human Rights*. A/HRC/RES/26/9. Geneva: OHCHR. Available at: www.ohchr.org/EN/HRBodies/HRC/WGTransCorp/Pages/IGWGOnTNC.aspx [Accessed 27 Sept. 2015].

Salomon, Margot E. (2007). *International Economic Governance and Human Rights Accountability*. LSE Law, Society and Economy Working Papers, 09-2007. London, UK: Department of Law, London School of Economics and Political Science.

Salomon, M. and Seiderman, I. (2012). Human rights norms for a globalized world: The Maastricht Principles on Extraterritorial Obligations of states in the area of economic, social, and cultural rights. *Global Policy* 3, pp. 458–62.

Sepúlveda, M. (2006). Obligations of 'international assistance and cooperation' in an optional protocol to the International Covenant on Economic, Social and Cultural Rights. *Netherlands Quarterly of Human Rights* 24(2), pp. 271–303.

Skogly, S. and Gibney, M. (2010). Introduction. In: M. Gibney and S. Skogly, eds., *Universal Human Rights and Extraterritorial Obligations*. Philadelphia: University of Pennsylvania Press, pp. 1–9.

Stiglitz, J. (2000). Capital market liberalization, economic growth, and instability. *World Development* 28, pp. 1075–86.

Stiglitz, J. (2008). Reversal of fortune. *Vanity Fair*. November. Available at: http://www.vanityfair.com/news/2008/11/stiglitz200811 [Accessed 27 Sept. 2015].

Swagel, P. (2009). *The Cost of the Economic Crisis: The Impact of the 2008 Economic Collapse. Pew Financial Reform Project, Briefing Paper 18*. Washington, DC: Pew Charitable Trusts. www.pewtrusts.org/uploadedFiles/wwwpewtrustsorg/Reports/Economic_Mobility/Cost-of-the-Crisis-final.pdf?n=6727 [Accessed 27 Sept. 2015].

8 Economic crises and human rights[1]

In autumn 2008, the full extent of the financial crisis became evident on Wall Street and in the City of London when five of the largest US investment banks failed or were on the verge of failure.[2] Trust between banks collapsed and they stopped lending to one another, leading to a lack of credit for businesses and households, not only in the US and UK but in many European countries. There were knock-on impacts on retail banks,[3] and the crisis threatened to precipitate a run on the banks. Immediate measures had to be taken by the governments of the US, the UK, and other European countries to rescue the global banking system. The credit squeeze led to a recession in the US, the UK, and most other European Union (EU) countries, and it led to sharp falls in the rate of growth of GDP in the rest of the world.

The financial crisis became an economic crisis, with rising rates of unemployment and poverty. The impact of this was felt particularly by many poor women who were required to increase their unpaid work to try to safeguard their families from the effects of poverty and unemployment (Balakrishnan, Elson, and Heintz 2011; Elson 2012). In 2009, the G20, a group of the twenty most powerful countries in the world—including India, China, South Africa, and Brazil—agreed on a coordinated fiscal stimulus composed of tax cuts and government expenditure in areas such as infrastructure. By 2010, there were signs of some recovery in output and employment. But the recession that resulted from the crisis had led to rising budget deficits, due to decreased tax revenues, higher spending from automatic stabilizers (such as unemployment insurance), and in some countries, the costs of stimulus packages. Some European countries (including Ireland, Spain, and Greece) had to pay much higher interest rates to borrow on international markets, which led to further increases in the deficit. In the course of 2010, fiscal stimulus in the EU gave way to fiscal austerity as public expenditure was drastically cut, plunging many countries into a second recession. The impact of the cuts to social security and public services was disproportionately felt by low income households as compared to high income households, women as compared to men, and by people from ethnic minorities as compared to those from the majority ethnic group (Elson 2013).

This chapter evaluates these events in the light of the human rights framework. It focuses on the obligation to protect in relation to financial regulation, drawing on the example of the US, and the obligation to fulfill in relation to fiscal stimulus and austerity, drawing on examples from Ireland, Spain, the UK, and Greece. It considers the discharge of these obligations in the light of the principles of progressive realization and non-retrogression, minimum core levels, non-discrimination and equality, and accountability, participation, and transparency. The analysis, though focused primarily on the 2008 global crisis in the US and Europe, can be applied to economic crises in general, such as those that have occurred in Asia, Argentina, and elsewhere. Although the specifics vary from one calamity to the next, human rights principles can be applied to interrogate the causes of economic crises, understand their effects and evaluate policy responses.

Financial crisis, financial regulation, and the obligation to protect

As discussed in other chapters, the obligation to protect requires governments to prevent violation of human rights by third parties. This means that the government must put in place an adequate system of regulation of private persons and businesses who might take actions that lead to violations of human rights. The financial sector has the potential to act in ways that support the progressive realization of economic and social rights or to act in ways that undermine the progressive realization of human rights. For instance, if the financial sector makes financing available to buy housing on terms that are non-discriminatory, i.e. affordable and stable, this can help the realization of the right to housing. However, if the financial sector makes financing available on terms that are discriminatory and potentially unaffordable and unstable, this can lead to retrogression in the enjoyment of the right to housing, especially if it contributes to the creation of financial crises that lead to foreclosure on mortgages and repossession of housing by financial companies (see Chapter 6).

The emergence of financial crisis is not a random shock originating from somewhere outside the economic and social system, but is created by the operation of institutions, both private sector institutions seeking to maximize profits, and by the regulatory behavior of public sector institutions. Appropriate regulation of the financial sector can limit the possibility of crisis and promote stability, but from 1980 onwards, governments with oversight of the major global financial centers changed the regulations, arguing that they were liberalizing financial markets to promote greater efficiency in the allocation of finance. These changes permitted financial institutions to engage in increasingly risky behavior.

For instance, in the US, between 1980 and 2002, Congress passed a series of laws that paved the way for the financial crisis of 2008 (Balakrishnan, Heintz, and Seguino 2009). The IMF has published research showing how US banks and other financial institutions lobbied Congress and donated money to politicians' election campaigns to secure these laws which enhanced their scope for making profits (Igan, Mishra, and Tressel 2009). These changes in the rights and obligations structuring the US financial system meant that many new financial products were virtually unregulated, including the mortgage-backed securities and credit default swaps that triggered the financial meltdown in the autumn of 2008. Banks had been allowed to borrow excessively against too little capital and to undertake risky innovations without any institution having an overview of how much risk was building up in the financial system as a whole. Many new financial assets, such as derivatives, were not traded in open markets but were traded over the counter to specific clients without any transparency or regulatory oversight. Looked at as a whole, the changes in regulation had strengthened the rights of the banks, made the system less transparent, and increased systemic risk.

By 2000, the US financial system was no longer robust. So long as the US Federal Reserve kept interest rates low, this was not readily apparent, but when it raised the Federal Funds interest rate to 5 percent in 2006 to combat inflation, this led to a rise in the interest that had to be paid on subprime mortgages, making monthly payments unaffordable. Banks had been allowed to use these mortgages as the basis for new securities that were globally traded, and these securities fell sharply in value, triggering a global financial crisis.

This chain of events had an immediate impact on Americans who had borrowed in the subprime market, disproportionately African Americans and single women, many of whom lost their homes (see Chapter 6; and also Balakrishnan, Elson, and Heintz 2011). The negative impact on the right to housing in the US was highlighted by the UN Special Rapporteur on the Right to Adequate Housing in her 2010 report, which identified, among a number of factors obstructing the realization of the right to housing, the problem of foreclosures (Rolnik 2010). She called for new legislation to create a national foreclosure prevention program, but as discussed in Chapter 6, there was far less government support for distressed borrowers than for distressed lenders, who were bailed out.

The ramifications of the financial crisis went far beyond the US housing market because US and European banks were forced to change their assessment of the risks of all the new financial products they had been trading, leading to a squeeze on credit for businesses, which in turn led to a substantial fall in output and employment across most of the developed countries. This jeopardized the realization of the right to an adequate standard of living as a whole, and also the right to work. There had clearly been a failure of the US government to protect economic and social rights.

The US government's measures to address the problems of the financial sector can be scrutinized from a human rights perspective (Balakrishnan, Heintz, and Seguino 2009). The US legislature authorized the US Treasury to spend up to $700 billion to prevent the collapse of banks through the Troubled Asset Relief Program (TARP), and by the end of 2009, $364 billion had been disbursed (US Department of the Treasury 2009), but there was a lack of transparency in the allocation of this money. The problem of transparency is even worse when considering the measures taken by the US Federal Reserve Bank to support the banking system through "quantitative easing," to make more finance available to the banks and other financial institutions, with no strings attached—no explicit requirements for banks to lend to businesses or to end the tradition of paying large annual bonuses to already highly paid executives or to ease the terms of mortgages for those having difficulty maintaining repayments. The details of these measures were not revealed, and the Federal Reserve enjoys important exemptions from the Freedom of Information Act. The Federal Advisory Council, which is composed of executives from leading banks, is allowed to meet with the Federal Reserve behind closed doors, and the Government Accountability Office is restricted in its ability to audit the Federal Reserve.

A human rights perspective emphasizes the question of whether the US government put in place measures to ensure that its obligation to protect would be met in future. A clear weakness is that most of the banks were able to stay under the same leadership that had so mismanaged them. Insolvent banks with government-guaranteed deposits were not placed under the control of the Federal Deposit Insurance Corporation (FDIC) despite the FDIC's existing powers of Prompt Corrective Action that were introduced in 1991 to deal with critically troubled banks. In July 2010, the US Congress did pass the Dodd-Frank Wall Street Reform and Consumer Protection Act that potentially gives the government a greater oversight role in financial markets. The provisions of the legislation include: the creation of new agencies to monitor system-wide risk among financial institutions, new procedures for liquidating federally insured institutions when they become insolvent, limitations on certain investment activities of banks, regulations on specific financial products which were virtually unregulated, and the establishment of a new bureau of consumer financial protection. This has been scrutinized from a human rights perspective by Balakrishnan, Elson, and Heintz (2011), who point out that while the Act provides authority to regulate, in many areas, it does not itself set specific standards.

To give a concrete example: the financial consumer protection agency, authorized by the Act, represents an effort to protect individuals from actions taken by financial institutions. The oversight role of the new agency is not restricted to the mortgage market, and includes credit cards, debit cards, other consumer loans, debt collection procedures, financial advisory services, and dispute settlement. The agency is meant to prevent the type of predatory lending and fraud that created the subprime mortgage crisis, requiring more stringent risk assessment and transparency. In principle, the new agency could play a pivotal role in regulating consumer credit. Nevertheless, its effectiveness will depend on how its new mandates are actually implemented in the future. Interests in the financial sector have strong incentives and sizeable resources at their disposal, to influence the key government bodies to minimize the impact of this new regulatory framework.

Several components of the Dodd-Frank Act support a human rights perspective to economic policy by reining in the power of major financial institutions and private businesses in the interest of the economy as a whole. The Consumer Financial Protection Bureau (CFPB) provides a central process for addressing regulation and oversight, eliminating any confusion over agency responsibility and streamlining means of enforcement. The Act also creates the Financial Stability Oversight Council, designed to monitor and make recommendations that will eliminate or mitigate risks that could lead to a future economic crash. The act limits commercial banks from participating in proprietary investing, which led to high-risk financial activity preceding the 2007–2009 recession.

A human rights framework provides an ethical discourse and a set of procedures that can strengthen efforts to make new regulatory measures more effective. For instance, the argument that human rights and financial regulation are interlinked excited considerable interest from the US Human Rights Network, which brings together many diverse grass roots social justice groups under the banner of claims for human rights; and activists undertook training on how they can incorporate issues like financial regulation into their work on the right to housing, the right to work and the right to health.

The issue of financial regulation was also raised in submissions to the United Nations Human Rights Council Universal Periodic Review of the US in both 2010 and 2014. The Center for Women's Global Leadership and the Political Economy Research Institute, in collaboration with others such as the Economic, Social and Cultural Rights Network (ESCR-Net), which links activists internationally, made submissions that called for the US government to introduce, domestically and in concert with other states, a comprehensive set of measures to prevent banks and other financial sector institutions from undermining the realization of human rights, to hold financial institutions accountable for the use of bailout funds and liquidity introduced into the US economy, and to increase transparency and accountability to ensure that the funds are being used to prevent the retrogression of rights (Center for Women's Global Leadership and the Political Economy Research Institute 2010 and 2014).

Fiscal stimulus and the obligation to fulfill economic and social rights

Bailing out the banks prevented depositors from losing their money, but did not prevent the drying up of credit, as banks used the money to build up their reserves (see Chapter 5). Bailing out the banks did not halt the rise in unemployment and fall in output, which were leading to deterioration in realization of many economic and social rights. In 2009 many governments introduced measures to stimulate production and employment through fiscal packages comprising increases in public expenditure and cuts to tax rates. For instance, in the US, the $787 billion fiscal stimulus was introduced in 2009: 28 to 30 percent of the increased expenditure went to state governments to enable them to support education and health provision in the face of declining tax revenues from business taxes and sales taxes.

Much of the remaining expenditures were used to fund government contracts, grants, and loans aimed at job creation, including in areas of infrastructure development and clean energy investments. Tax cuts constituted about 35 percent of the total stimulus and were supposed to encourage people to spend more, and thus support jobs in that way.

This stimulus was part of a series of coordinated measures undertaken by a newly formed G20 group of developed and developing countries to try to offset the credit squeeze and prevent a global depression on the scale of the 1930s. At the London G20 summit in April 2009, the member governments agreed on a $5 trillion dollar fiscal expansion, pledged an extra $1.1 trillion of resources for global institutions, primarily the IMF, and promised to reform the banks (Elliott 2011). This intervention did prevent the crisis from being followed by a global depression. Although the economies of many of the developed countries went into recession, the recession was not as deep as it would otherwise have been; and while growth slowed down in the developing country members of the G20, they did not experience a recession.

From a human rights perspective the G20 initiative can or should be seen as an important contribution towards the obligation to fulfill rights. However, we also need to look at the design of such programs, including the balance between tax cuts and extra spending. Tax cuts that put more purchasing power into the hands of the poor and middle class—through a cut in VAT for example—are more compatible with a human rights perspective than reducing income and other taxes for the richest groups. The stimulus measures were successful in counteracting the recessionary impact of the financial crisis and by 2010 there were signs of recovery in output and employment.

From stimulus to austerity in EU countries

The period of stimulus in the EU was very short lived. Bailing out banks added to the liabilities of governments. Moreover, the recession that the stimulus packages were meant to address had caused increases in budget deficits as a result of the fall in government tax revenues; and in so far as the stimulus packages included tax reductions, they contributed to a further increase in deficits in the short run. Governments needed to borrow more to finance these deficits, and this created particular problems for some of the governments that had to borrow in a currency they did not control, as is the case for those European governments that are members of the Eurozone.[4]

Before the financial crisis, the costs of servicing public debt did not differ much between Eurozone governments. But after the crisis, private sector financial institutions responded by charging a higher price to hold the bonds of several EU countries, mainly in the Mediterranean, and the ratings given to their bonds were downgraded.[5] In the case of Ireland, the reason for higher interest payments can be attributed to the Irish banking crisis, and the massive bailout of Irish banks. An independent audit of the Irish debt found that when the contingent liabilities are counted, the Irish national debt stood at €371.1 billion on 31 March 2011, equivalent to almost 300 percent of Irish national income. Of this, €279.3 billion (over 75 percent) is accounted for by the state-covered debts of the Irish banks. As the audit puts it, "it is clear that the bulk of Irish government debt has arisen directly from the banking crisis, the decision in September 2008 to rescue all of the Irish banks" (Killian, Garvey, and Shaw 2011).

In the case of Greece, with a change of government, an important role was played by the publication in 2009 of new information on the fiscal position that showed a larger budget deficit and a higher debt-to-GDP ratio than previously thought. There were also problems in the Greek banking system, which had massively expanded loans to the private sector in the period 2001–2007. Both private and public debt in Germany and France were also heavily exposed to Greek debt (Blustein 2015).

Increased costs of government borrowing did not simply reflect increased government debt-to-GDP ratios. Consider Germany and Spain. In 2000 the debt-to-GDP ratio of Germany was 61 percent and in 2010 it was 77 percent; the ratio of Spain was 71 percent in 2000 and 72 percent in 2010. In 2008, the cost of borrowing was much the same for both countries, at around 4 percent. Yet while the cost of borrowing fell for Germany, to around 2 percent in early 2011, for Spain it rose to around 6 percent in early 2011.[6] It seems that the financial markets had changed their assessments of the risks of lending to different countries in the Eurozone. It has been suggested that in some cases they were also factoring in the ratio of private debt to GDP, in the expectation that where it was high, governments would have to spend more money in further bailouts for the banks. In Germany, private indebtedness had not increased in relation to GDP, standing at 165 percent in 2000, and 164 percent in 2010. But in Spain, private indebtedness had increased from 187 percent in 2000 to 283 percent in 2010.[7]

Whatever the origins, increased rates of interest led to a sovereign debt crisis in Ireland, Greece and Portugal,[8] with ramifications for the Eurozone as a whole. The European financial sector (especially large German and French banks) held large amounts of this sovereign debt, and the sector's stability was directly threatened by the possibility of default. Unlike the US situation, in which the Federal Reserve orchestrated support for the financial sector via buying mortgage-backed securities, the European Central Bank (ECB) refused in 2010 to support governments by buying significant amounts of sovereign debt. Instead, the ECB primarily focused on stabilizing the European financial sector by providing loans (along with the Eurozone Finance Ministers and the IMF) to governments. Conditions were attached to the loans, requiring large cuts to government spending, privatization of public assets, cuts to pensions, and reductions of workers' rights.[9]

Doubts were also cast over the finances of Spain, and austerity policies were introduced by the government, with the aim of averting a sovereign debt crisis. The UK is not a member of the Eurozone and did not experience a debt crisis of the kind experienced by Mediterranean Europe, but the coalition government that came to power in May 2010 decided that reducing the budget deficit and debt-to-GDP ratios must have top priority and subsequently introduced extensive expenditure cuts. These drastic cuts were described by the UK Minister of Finance, the Chancellor of the Exchequer, as "unavoidable" in order to earn "credibility in international markets" (Elson 2012, p. 177).

Austerity policies and obligations to fulfill economic and social rights

Some economists (and governments) argued that the austerity policies would be an "expansionary contraction," as they would restore confidence in the financial markets, and stimulate private investment which would lead to a recovery.[10] This turned out to be completely mistaken, and the austerity policies led to a second recession in 2012 in a large number of EU countries, including Austria, the Netherlands, and the UK, as well as Italy, Spain, Portugal and Greece. Even Germany, the strongest economy, achieved no more than a 0.2 percent increase in output in the third quarter of 2012 (Elliott and Moulds 2012). Financial crisis had been followed by ongoing broad-based economic crisis in many EU countries, with very high levels of unemployment, especially among the young, and increases in poverty and inequality (Elson 2013). Women were hard hit by cuts to public services, especially care services and health services (European Women's Lobby 2012).

Some economists have been very critical of the austerity policies in the EU, arguing that the way to deal with large budget deficits and high debt-to-GDP ratios is through policies that promote economic growth, particularly through public investment in infrastructure. Economic growth, it is argued, would in the medium term bring down unemployment and increase tax revenue by more than public expenditure, reducing budget deficits and reducing debt-to-GDP ratios.

Examining austerity policies from a human rights perspective deepens the critique by pointing out that not all forms of economic growth contribute to human well-being and emphasizing the objective of realization of economic and social rights. It foregrounds the human rights obligations of finance ministers, which must take precedence over other obligations, such as to creditors. A human rights perspective requires that the avoidance of retrogression in the realization of human rights must be at the forefront of the design of policies to deal with financial and economic crisis. In addition, governments have an immediate obligation to provide the minimum core of economic and social rights to safeguard the most deprived; and to ensure that there is compliance with the principle of equality and non-discrimination in the design of policy response. A human rights perspective provides an ethical framework that contests money-based discourses of morality that insist that debtors are always morally bound to pay their debts and that the bailouts are subject to "moral hazard"; and contests discourses that characterize working-age people who are in receipt of out-of-work benefits as "shirkers" and "frauds."

In May 2012, human rights considerations were drawn to the attention of governments of states that were party to the ICESCR in a letter from the Chair of CESCR, which says that in the context of economic crisis:

> Any proposed policy change or adjustment has to meet the following requirements: First, the policy is a temporary measure covering the period of crisis only; second, the policy is necessary and proportionate, in the sense that the adoption of any other policy, or failure to act, would be more detrimental to economic, social and cultural rights; third, the policy is not discriminatory and comprises all possible measures, including tax measures, to support social transfers to mitigate inequalities that can grow in times of crisis and to ensure that the rights of disadvantaged and marginalised individuals and groups are not disproportionately affected; fourth, the policy identifies the minimum core content of rights, or a social protection floor, as developed by the International Labour Organisation, and ensures the protection of this core content at all times.
>
> (Pillay 2012)

The issue of safeguarding human rights in times of economic crisis has also been taken up by the Human Rights Commissioner of the Council of Europe[11] in a paper that sets out a series of concrete recommendations for human rights-compliant responses to the crisis and addresses the important and unique role of national human rights structures in ensuring that human rights are safeguarded in the crisis context (Commissioner for Human Rights, Council of Europe 2013). The report found setbacks in the realization of the right to work, the right to an adequate standard of living, the right to social security, the right to housing, the right to food, the right to education, and the right to health. Existing inequalities were being exacerbated. Among the recommendations were that governments should conduct systematic human rights and equality impact assessments of social and economic policies and budgets:

> Ex ante and ex post facto assessments should gauge the present and future impacts of austerity measures and budgets on the enjoyment of human rights. Audits of fiscal policy should evaluate whether fiscal contractions are strictly necessary by identifying all possible resourcing alternatives. Austerity measures should not be discriminatory and they should remain temporary, covering only the period of the crisis. Funding levels have to be restored when more resources become available.
> (Commissioner for Human Rights, Council of Europe 2013, p. 9)

While ministers of finance have not done much to heed these calls, the human rights framework has proved a useful resource in trying to build coalitions to resist austerity policies. Here we look at examples for Ireland, Spain, the UK, and Greece.

The government of Ireland had to agree to reduce its budget deficit from 11.7 percent of GDP in 2010 to less than 3 percent in 2015, as a condition for loans from the EU and IMF in 2010. It chose to make two-thirds of the reduction via reductions in public expenditure and one-third through tax raising measures (Government of Ireland 2010). Cuts were made to the funding for the Irish Human Rights Commission, the Equality Authority, the Ombudsman for Children, and the National Disability Authority. A large number of welfare benefits have been cut: child benefit, carer's allowance, one parent family payment, disability payment, rent subsidy, and jobseeker's allowance. There have been substantial cuts to the budgets for health, education and skills, children and youth, and disability projects. A cut to the minimum wage was planned, but this was overturned by a new government that came to power in March 2011 (Barry and Conroy 2013). A new Programme for Government and National Recovery 2011–2016 was produced which delayed the achievement of the 3 percent target until 2015 and sought to renegotiate the terms of the EU/ IMF loan to reduce interest payments. However, the broad direction of policy was retained.

The UN Independent Expert on Human Rights and Extreme Poverty, Magdalena Sepúlveda Carmona, undertook a mission to Ireland, publishing a report in May 2011 (Carmona 2011). She expressed concern that:

> Ireland did not undertake any meaningful efforts to ensure a broad national dialogue, with effective and meaningful participation of civil society and members of the public, when formulating its budgetary responses to the crises, and entering into the EU/IMF loan. This is particularly so given that a number of well-designed participatory mechanisms are already in place in Ireland which allow for the voices of the most vulnerable to be taken into account in the formulation of policy. Failure to ensure participation and transparency in the design of national policies seriously jeopardizes the State's ability to respond to its human rights obligations, undermines the effectiveness of budgetary adjustment policies, and prevents the needs of the poorest and most excluded from being taken into account.
>
> (para 37)

She welcomed the new government's commitment to making the budget process fully transparent and open to public scrutiny going forward, and encouraged the utilization, support, and strengthening of permanent structures and pathways for consultation with individuals, civil society, trade unions, community organizations, grassroots movements, and the academic community (Ibid., para 37).

As discussed in Chapter 3, the independent expert took as the standard of poverty used by the government of Ireland—that households are living in poverty if their income and resources are low enough to prevent them from having a standard of living which is acceptable by Irish society (Carmona 2011, para 14). Against this benchmark, she found that cuts to social security and public services posed a threat to the enjoyment of human rights by the most vulnerable sectors of society, especially children, older persons, persons with disabilities, single parents, the Traveller community, migrants, asylum-seekers and refugees, and homeless people. She noted that while the government is entitled to decide the scale and pace of adjustments, the decision to achieve adjustments primarily through expenditure cuts rather than tax increases had major implications for the fulfillment of its economic, social, and cultural rights obligations. Reductions in public expenditure affect the poorest and most vulnerable with the most severity, whereas some increase in taxation could place the burden on those who are better equipped to cope (Ibid., para 24).

The independent expert concluded that:

> While Ireland has made impressive advances in poverty reduction over the past decade, these gains will be reversed if those living in poverty and social exclusion are not protected during the recovery.

The crises provide an opportunity for Ireland to put human rights at the heart of the recovery, and to meet some of its long-standing social goals. The burden of the crises must be shared by all segments of Irish society, while those living in poverty and social exclusion must be protected as a matter of priority.

(Ibid., para 95)

NGOs in Ireland followed up this report by engaging with two Universal Periodic Reviews of Ireland by the UN Human Rights Council, in 2011 and 2015, submitting a stakeholders report based on extensive consultations (http://www.rightsnow.ie).

In Spain, a coalition of NGOs[12] took advantage of Spain's appearance in May 2012 before the UN Committee on Economic, Social and Cultural Rights to present a parallel report providing detailed evidence of retrogressions in human rights due to austerity measures. In the review session, the Committee raised many of the concerns raised in the shadow report with the government, probing in particular the human rights impacts of recent budget cuts, reforms to labor and health practices, and housing foreclosures and evictions, as well as ongoing discrimination against women and the Gitano (Roma) community.

The shadow report drew on a factsheet providing a statistical snapshot of the deterioration of economic and social rights in Spain produced by the Center for Economic and Social Rights.[13] The factsheet (CESR 2012) notes that although these rights are guaranteed in the Spanish Constitution as "guiding principles" to inform public decisions, the austerity measures were undertaken without prior assessment of their human rights impact or their distributional effects on particularly vulnerable groups. In the face of pressures to reduce Spain's fiscal deficit, austerity measures have primarily cut spending on social sectors such as education, housing, social security and international development cooperation. There has been an upward trend in poverty and inequality in Spain. Unemployment has climbed to extreme levels, with a quarter of the labor force out of work and youth unemployment at around fifty percent. Moreover, statistics highlight stark disparities on grounds of gender, age, nationality, geography and socio-economic status. The factsheet shows how expenditure cuts measures have jeopardized the right to work and to decent working conditions, the right to housing, and the right to an adequate standard of living. It notes that austerity measures have focused almost exclusively on cuts in public expenditure rather than on increasing revenue through progressive tax reforms aimed at ensuring that the wealthiest sectors of the population contribute their share, including reducing tax evasion. It points out that in 2011–2012, there were cuts of €27.3 billion, compared to estimated losses of tax revenue of €88 billion due to evasion in 2010, mainly by large companies and rich individuals.

Through the efforts of the NGOs, newspapers, radio and television programs, and internet news sites from all over Spain and as far afield as Argentina and Mexico reported on the session in which Spain was reviewed and conducted interviews with representatives of CESR and the other NGOs present. In its concluding observations, the Committee calls on Spain to review austerity measures which are causing "disproportionate" harm to the most vulnerable and marginalized groups and individuals, especially those living in poverty, women, children, persons with disabilities, and unemployed persons—particularly youth, homeless persons, the Roma community, migrants, and asylum-seekers. Furthermore, the Committee reminds the state that it is precisely in times of economic crisis when efforts must be redoubled to guarantee human rights for everyone, without discrimination, and in particular for the most vulnerable (Comité de Derechos Económicos, Sociales y Culturales 2012).

The UK did not face any sovereign debt problems but nevertheless the coalition government that came to power in May 2010 introduced a so-called "emergency" budget in June 2010 that set out a strategy for rapid reduction of the UK budget deficit. Reductions in expenditure were to achieve 77 percent of the proposed fiscal consolidation, and rises in tax revenue 23 percent. The UK has ratified all the UN international human rights treaties and has also set up an Equalities and Human Rights Commission with a statutory remit to promote and monitor human rights and to protect, enforce, and promote equality across the nine "protected" grounds—age, disability, gender, race, religion and belief, pregnancy and maternity, marriage and civil partnership, sexual orientation, and gender reassignment. The official government manual on appraisal and evaluation in central government (HM Treasury 2003) does make a brief reference to the Human Rights Act (Ibid., p. 9), and to the Convention on the Elimination of All Forms of Discrimination against Women, the Convention on the Elimination of All Forms of Racial Discrimination, the International Covenant on Civil and Political Rights, and the International Covenant on Economic, Social and Cultural Rights (Ibid., p. 95). However, no detailed guidance is given. It is merely stated that these should inform the development of policy. The limited impact assessments that were provided for the June 2010 budget did not mention human rights.

Elson (2012) considers the deficit reduction strategy in the light of CEDAW obligations, citing evidence produced by researchers at the House of Commons Library on the distribution between women and men of the £8 billion raised by the changes in direct taxes and benefits introduced in the June 2010 budget that finds that £5.8 billion will be paid by women and only £2.2 billion by men. She also cites the verdict on the June 2010 budget from the UK Women's Budget Group[14] that "while the budget has a few individual measures that help to offset gender inequality, such as . . . the exemption of low income workers from the public sector pay freeze, the budget taken as a whole is likely unfair in its impact on women as compared to men" (UK Women's Budget Group 2010, p. 2). Subsequent analysis of the combined impact of budget measures, including changes to taxes and cuts to social security benefits and public services, found that single women are particularly hard hit (UK Women's Budget Group 2013). In relation to their total income, including imputed income in kind from use of public services as well as cash income, single mothers lose the most: 15.6 percent, compared to single fathers who lose 11.7 percent and couples with children who lose 9.7 percent. Among pensioners, it is single women pensioners who lose most: 12.5 percent, compared to single male pensioners who lose 9.5 percent and couple pensioners who lose 8.6 percent. Among working age families with no children, single women lose 10.9 percent, single men lose 9.0 percent and couples lose 4.1 percent.

There has been a growing civil society movement in the UK to examine the cuts in terms of their impact on human rights, with studies by local groups in the cities of Coventry and Bristol (Harrison and Stephenson 2011; Mapson 2011). The Trades Union Congress published a handbook explaining the methods used in these studies, and how trade unions and civil society organizations can use them to conduct similar assessments in other places (Trades Union Congress 2011). The impact of the cuts on women's rights was highlighted in the shadow report submitted by UK women's groups to the CEDAW Committee in 2013 on the occasion of the review of the UK's 7th Periodic Report (Women's Resource Centre 2013). The CEDAW Committee, in Concluding Observations on the 7th Periodic report, expressed concern about the impact of the cuts on women and urged the UK government to mitigate this impact (CEDAW 2013, paras 21 and 22).

The economic crisis in the EU has been the worst in Greece. By 2014, output was down about 26 percent; unemployment was at 25.8 percent, with youth unemployment at 49.6 percent; and nominal wages had fallen by 23.5 percent (Weisbrot, Rosnick, and Lefebvre 2015). Access to health care was particularly hard hit, as the bailout in 2010 stipulated big cuts in spending and structural reforms for the health sector. Many people saw their health insurance entitlements reduced and health provision cut, and as a result there were large increases in unmet medical needs, a marked worsening of mental health, and a sharp deterioration in the health status of vulnerable groups, particularly drug users and migrants. By the end of 2014, nearly a quarter of the Greek population lacked health insurance (Kentikelenis 2015).

The bailout in 2010 changed the debt profile, but worsened the overall debt situation. Greek bonds held by European and Greek banks were sold at record levels causing public debt that had been held privately to be transferred to other Eurozone member states and the IMF. The share of bonds in total Greek debt decreased from 91.1 percent in 2009 to 70.5 percent in 2011, while the share of loans increased from 5.2 percent in 2009 to 25.3 percent in 2011. Between the end of 2009 and the end of 2011 sovereign debt increased by more than 18 percent, from €299 billion to €355 billion (Truth Committee on Public Debt 2015, p. 20). A second bailout was required in 2012, which included some debt restructuring, a cut in the nominal value of bonds held by private bondholders, and intensified conditions demanding more austerity. This did not resolve the debt problem, and by 2014 debt was 177.1 percent of GDP, compared to 129.7 percent in 2010, and the share of loans was 73 percent, mainly owed to the European Financial Stability Facility (Ibid.). The strategy of the creditors has been described as "pretend and extend."

An anti-austerity government came to power in early 2015, and the new President of the Greek Parliament set up the Truth Committee on Public Debt, an independent committee of experts from 11 countries, to examine Greek government debt, including the extent to which it had been incurred in compliance with human rights principles. Their report cited the UN Guiding Principles on Foreign Debt and Human Rights (see Chapter 5), endorsed by the UN Human Rights Council in 2012 (UN doc. A.HRC/20/23) which state that:

> All States have the obligation to respect, protect and fulfil human rights. In this regard, they should ensure that any or all of their activities concerning their lending and borrowing decisions, those of international, national, public or private institutions to which they belong or in which they have an interest, the negotiation and implementation of loan agreements or other debt instruments, the utilization of loan funds, debt repayments, the renegotiation and restructuring of external debt, and the provision of debt relief when appropriate, do not derogate from these obligations.
>
> (para 6)

> International organizations have an obligation to respect human rights. This implies a duty to refrain from formulating, adopting, funding and implementing policies and programmes which directly or indirectly contravene the enjoyment of human rights.
>
> (para 9)

> States should ensure that their rights and obligations arising from external debt agreements or arrangements do not hinder the progressive realization of economic, social and cultural rights.
>
> (para 16)

The Committee concludes that Greece was effectively coerced into violating fundamental human rights obligations through the bailout conditions and points out that sovereign creditors have an obligation not to frustrate or force another party to violate its obligations. No state can legitimately claim to be discharging its own human rights obligations territorially while at the same time actively pressuring another state to violate its own obligations (Truth Committee on Public Debt 2015, p. 59).

Conclusions

It is clear that if governments had complied with their human rights obligations to protect by effective regulation of the financial sector, there would not have been a financial crisis in 2008. Even after the financial crisis emerged, it would not have led to a widespread economic crisis in many EU countries, with retrogression in the enjoyment of many economic and social rights, if governments and international organizations had designed their response in line with human rights obligations to fulfill economic and social rights. It is clear that governments in Ireland, Spain, and the UK could have made more equitable efforts to generate resources through raising more tax revenue as an alternative to cuts to spending on public social services, in line with their obligation to employ the maximum of available resources towards the realization of economic, social, and cultural rights, without discrimination or retrogression. It is clear that the creditors of Greece could have found a sustainable and human rights compliant solution to the problem of Greek sovereign debt through measures to write off a much bigger proportion of the debt. By providing an alternative evaluative framework and a set of procedures which civil society organizations could utilize in mobilizing for social justice, a human rights framework strengthens the critique of the economic policies that led to the financial crisis of 2008 and turned the crisis, at least in several EU countries, into a longer-term economic collapse.

Notes

1 Portions of this chapter incorporate material from a previously published article. Radhika Balakrishnan, Diane Elson, and James Heintz (2011). Financial regulation, capabilities and human rights in the US financial crisis: The case of housing. *Journal of Human Development and Capabilities* 12(1), pp. 153–68. Reprinted with permission.
2 The precise dating of the economic and financial crisis varies. Some argue that it began in 2007, when the extent of the subprime mortgage crisis became clear. For the purposes of this chapter, we use a starting year of 2008, when the global reach of the crisis became clear.
3 A retail bank deals directly with consumers and primarily deals with checking and savings accounts, mortgages, and personal loans. An investment bank, on the other hand, raises money by selling securities to companies and to the government, and provides advice to corporations about mergers and buyouts.
4 The members of the EU are Austria, Belgium, Bulgaria, Cyprus, Czech Republic, Denmark, Estonia, Finland, France, Germany, Greece, Hungary, Ireland, Italy, Latvia, Lithuania, Luxembourg, Malta, Netherlands, Poland, Portugal, Romania, Slovakia, Slovenia, Spain, Sweden, and the United

Kingdom. Of these, the following are NOT members of the Eurozone: Bulgaria, Czech Republic, Denmark, Hungary, Poland, Romania, Sweden, and the United Kingdom.

5 Government bonds are rated by three US based privately owned ratings agencies: Standard and Poor's, Moody's, and the much smaller Fitch. The top rating is AAA. The higher the rating, the cheaper it is for governments to borrow.

6 For data, see "What really caused the Eurozone crisis?" Available at: www. bbc.co.uk/news/business [Accessed 1 Dec. 2012].

7 For data, see "What really caused the Eurozone crisis?" Available at: www. bbc.co.uk/news/business [Accessed 1 Dec. 2012].

8 Unfortunately there is no space to discuss Portugal here.

9 This policy changed in summer 2012, when, in the context of a possibility that Spain would need a bailout, the Governor of the ECB announced he would do 'whatever it takes' to save the euro (Black and Randow 2012).

10 The argument that government cutbacks can stimulate growth is often referred to as the expansionary fiscal contraction hypothesis—originally based on case studies of Denmark and Ireland. The validity of the hypothesis remains questionable. The seminal paper on expansionary fiscal contractions is Giavazzi and Pagano (1990).

11 The Council of Europe is the continent's leading human rights organization. It includes 47 member states, 28 of which are members of the European Union. All Council of Europe member states have signed up to the European Convention on Human Rights, a treaty designed to protect human rights, democracy and the rule of law. The European Court of Human Rights oversees the implementation of the Convention in the member states.

12 The coalition brought together a range of human rights, development, health, and social justice organizations, including those working on the rights of children, women, people with disabilities, LGBT people, and the Gitano community.

13 For information about the Center for Economic and Social Rights, which has its office in New York, see http://www.cesr.org/.

14 The UK Women's Budget Group is a network of academic researchers, policy officers in trade unions and women's organizations, and activists. It critically analyzes the budgets of the UK government, including both taxation and expenditure. It calls for an alternative macroeconomic policy that would be more gender equitable. Diane Elson has served as Chair of the WBG since 2010. See www.wbg.org.uk.

References

Balakrishnan, R., Heintz, J., and Seguino, S. (2009). *A Human Rights Response to the Economic Crisis in the US*. New Brunswick, NJ: Center for Women's Global Leadership, Rutgers University.

Balakrishnan, R., Elson, D., and Heintz, J. (2011). Financial regulation, capabilities and human rights in the US financial crisis: The case of housing. *Journal of Human Development and Capabilities* 12(1), pp. 153–68.

Barry, U. and Conroy, P. (2013). Ireland in crisis: Women, austerity and inequality. In: M. Karamessini and J. Rubery, eds., *Women and Austerity: The Economic Crisis and the Future for Gender Equality*. London: Routledge, pp. 186–206.

Black, J. and Randow, J. (2012). Draghi says ECB will do what's needed to preserve Euro. *Bloomberg*. 26 July. Available at: http://www.bloomberg.com/news/

articles/2012-07-26/draghi-says-ecb-to-do-whatever-needed-as-yields-threaten-europe [accessed 30 Aug. 2015].

Blustein, P. (2015). *Laid Low: The IMF, the Euro Zone and the First Rescue of Greece. Cigi Papers No. 61.* Available at: https://goo.gl/lvRKFE [Accessed 12 June 2015].

Carmona, M. (2011). *Report of Independent Expert on Question of Human Rights and Extreme Poverty: Mission to Ireland.* UN Document: A/HRC/17/34/Add.2.

Center for Economic and Social Rights (CESR). (2012). Spain, Fact Sheet No. 12. Available at: http://www.cesr.org/downloads/FACT%20SHEET%20SPAIN. pdf.

Center for Women's Global Leadership and the Political Economy Research Institute. (2010). *Towards a Human Rights-Centred Macroeconomic and Financial Policy in the U.S. 2010.* [Submission to the United Nations Human Rights Council]. Available at: http://cwgl.rutgers.edu/docman/universal-periodic-review-upr/461-may-2010-macro-econ-report-us-upr-2/file [Accessed 6 Sept. 2010].

Center for Women's Global Leadership and the Political Economy Research Institute. (2014). *Towards a Human Rights-Centred Macroeconomic and Financial Policy in the U.S. Revisited. 2014.* [Submission to the United Nations Human Rights Council]. Available at: http://cwgl.rutgers.edu/docman/economic-and-social-rights-publications/696-cwgl-peri-upr-review-stakeholder-report/ file [Accessed 6 Sept. 2015].

Comité de Derechos Económicos, Sociales y Culturales. (2012). *Examen de los informes presentados por los Estados partes en virtud de los artículos 16 y 17 del Pacto Observaciones finales del Comité de Derechos Económicos, Sociales y Culturales.* E/C.12/ESP/CO/5.

Commissioner for Human Rights, Council of Europe. (2013). *Safeguarding Human Rights in Times of Economic Crisis.* Strasbourg: Council of Europe. Available at: https://wcd.coe.int/com.instranet.InstraServlet?command=com.instranet. CmdBlobGet&InstranetImage=2664103&SecMode=1&DocId=2215366&Us age=2 [Accessed 22 Sept. 2015].

Committee on the Elimination of All Discrimination against Women (CEDAW). (2013). *Concluding Observations on the Seventh Periodic Report of the United Kingdom of Great Britain and Northern Ireland.* UN Document: CEDAW/C/GBR/ CO/7.

Elliott, L. (2011). Global financial crises: Five key stages 2007–2011. *Guardian,* 7 August. Available at: http://www.theguardian.com/business/2011/aug/07/ global-financial-crisis-key-stages [Accessed 30 Sept. 2015].

Elliott, L. and Moulds, J. (2012). Double-dip brings recession confirmed in Eurozone. *Guardian,* 16 November. Available at: http://www.theguardian. com/business/2012/nov/15/eurozone-double-dip-recession [Accessed 27 Sept. 2015].

Elson, D. (2012). The reduction of the UK budget deficit: A human rights perspective, *International Review of Applied Economics* 26(2), pp. 177–90.

Elson, D. (2013). Economic crises from the 1980s to the 2010s: A gender analysis. In G. Waylen and S. Rai, eds., *New Frontiers in Feminist Political Economy.* London: Routledge, pp. 189–212.

European Women's Lobby (EWL). (2012). The Price of Austerity: The Impact on Women's Rights and Gender Equality in Europe. Available at: www.womenlobby.org [Accessed 1 Dec. 2012].

Giavazzi, F. and Pagano, M. (1990). Can severe fiscal contractions be expansionary? Tales of two small European countries. In O. J. Blanchard and S. Fischer, eds., *NBER Macroeconomics Annual 1990, Volume 5*. Cambirdge, MA: MIT Press, pp. 75–122.

Government of Ireland. (2010) *National Recovery Plan 2011–14*. Available at: http://www.budget.gov.ie/RecoveryPlan.aspx.

Harrison, J. and Stephenson, M.A. (2011). *Unravelling Equality: A Human Rights and Equality Impact Assessment of the Public Sector Spending Cuts on Women in Coventry*. Conventry: Centre of Human Rights in Practice and Coventry Women's Voices.

HM Treasury. (2003). *The Green Book: Appraisal and Evaluation in Central Government*. London: TSO.

Igan, D., Mishra, P., and Tressel, T. (2009). *A Fistful of Dollars: Lobbying and the Financial Crisis. IMF Working Paper WP/09/287*. Washington, DC: IMF.

Kentikelenis, A. (2015). Is this the moment Greece's suffering starts to ease? *New Scientist*. Available at: https://www.newscientist.com/article/dn27034-is-this-the-moment-greeces-suffering-starts-to-ease/# [Accessed 27 Sept. 2015].

Killian, S., Garvey, J., and Shaw, F. (2011). *An Audit of Irish Debt*. Limerick: University of Limerick. Available at: http://www.debtireland.org/download/pdf/audit_of_irish_debt6.pdf [Accessed 27 Sept. 2015].

Mapson, A. (2011). *Cutting Women Out in Bristol: A Report of the Human Rights and Equality Impact Assessment of the Public Sector Spending Cuts on Women in Bristol*. Bristol: Fawcett Society Bristol Local Group. Available at: http://www.bristolfawcett.org.uk/wp-content/uploads/2015/02/BristolCuttingWomen Out.pdf [Accessed 27 Sept. 2015].

Pillay, G. (2012). *Chairperson, Committee on Economic, Social and Cultural Rights. Document*. CESCR/48th/SP/MAB/SW.

Rolnik, R. (2010). *Report of the Special Rapporteur on Adequate Housing, as a Component of the Right to an Adequate Standard of Living and the Right to Non-Discrimination in this Context. Human Rights Council*. Document: A/HRC/13/20/Add 4.

Trades Union Congress. (2011). Women and the Cuts Toolkit. Available at: www.tuc.org.uk/equality/tuc-20286-f0.cfm. [Accessed 27 Sept. 2015].

Truth Committee on Public Debt. (2015). *Preliminary Report, Hellenic Parliament*. Available at: http://www.hellenicparliament.gr/UserFiles/f3c70a23-7696-49db-9148-f24dce6a27c8/Report_web.pdf. [Accessed 27 Sept. 2015].

UK Women's Budget Group. (2010). A gender impact assessment of the coalition government budget, June. Available at: http://www.wbg.org.uk. [Accessed 27 Sept. 2015].

UK Women's Budget Group. (2013). To ensure economic recovery for women, we need Plan F. Available at: http://www.wbg.org.uk/wp-content/uploads/2013/10/WBG-briefing_Sept-2013_final.pdf [Accessed 27 Sept. 2015].

United States Senate Committee on Banking, Housing, and Urban Affairs. (2010). *Brief Summary of the Dodd-Frank Wall Street Reform and Consumer Protection Act*. Available at: http://www.banking.senate.gov/public/_files/070110_Dodd_Frank_Wall_Street_Reform_comprehensive_summary_Final.pdf [Accessed 22 Sept. 2015].

UN Human Rights Council. (2012). *UN Guiding Principles on Foreign Debt and Human Rights.* UN Document A.HRC/20/23.

US Department of the Treasury. (2009). *Agency Financial Report (Office of Financial Stability) Fiscal Year 2009.* Washington, DC: US Department of the Treasury.

Weisbrot, M., Rosnick, D., and Lefebvre, S. (2015). *The Greek Economy: Which Way Forward?* Washington, DC: Center for Economic and Policy Research.

Women's Resource Centre. (2013). *Women's Equality in the UK: A Health Check.* London: Women's Resource Centre.

Conclusion

This book has argued that the human rights approach constitutes an alternative ethical framework for assessing economic outcomes. It provides a basis for interrogating the role of the institutions in society—from the state to markets to corporations—in contributing to, or undermining, progress towards social justice. Applying human rights principles and obligations transforms economic policy-making, grounding it in the substantive freedoms that all people should enjoy. It embraces a vision of a democratic economy, where societies deliberate about what is most important, while guaranteeing core protections for the vulnerable and the disadvantaged. It challenges hierarchies and asymmetries of power and privilege among the world's countries.

As first discussed in Chapter 1, Article 28 of the Universal Declaration of Human Rights (UDHR) states that "everyone is entitled to a social and international order in which the rights and freedoms set forth in this Declaration can be fully realized." The current social and international order falls far short of this ideal. But, given the ideas explored in this book, what would this new social order actually look like?

The new social order would be one committed to substantive equality—where all people enjoy the same rights, evaluated in terms of actual, realized outcomes. Do people have the freedom to learn? Can they reasonably expect to live long and healthy lives? Will they have a standard of living that allows them to feel fully part of society, without fear of poverty and deprivation? Are they able to be productive and work in decent jobs with dignity? Can they go through their day without worrying about their safety or their families' safety?

This book has tried to identify elements of this new social order—those pieces of the larger puzzle that determine how well our economy does in securing the enjoyment of basic rights. The human rights approach implies that there should be a distribution of income and wealth consistent with the realization of rights. This includes a fundamental commitment to non-discrimination and equality across gender, race, ethnicity, caste, sexuality, and other dimensions. It requires an approach to the allocation of resources in ways that support the realization of rights, using policy instruments such as public spending, taxation, government borrowing, and monetary policy, with the objective of improving people's lives, not simply promoting faster growth.

The new order must provide mechanisms to hold the state to account in terms of the formulation of policies and the use of resources to respect, protect, and fulfill rights. This includes fostering a vibrant and participatory democracy. It must be able to discipline the actions of finance and transnational corporations and correct power imbalances in the economy. It must be able to manage the uncertainties of the world we live in, reducing volatility and giving people the wherewithal to navigate the risks they face. It is a truly global order with effective international governance that supports meaningful coordination between countries to support the realization of rights and prevent powerful countries pursuing policies that impede the realization of rights elsewhere.

But why human rights? What does a framework for social justice based on rights get us? Where is the value added? As we have argued, the human rights approach gives a normative framework based on a theory of social justice that is richer than that found in much of modern economic thinking. Human rights is clear about what economic policy is really for—it's about people's lives—and it provides alternatives to economic growth and low inflation as the primary goals we should strive to achieve. It provides a grounded way of evaluating and assessing policy alternatives that is far richer than techniques that ostensibly quantify costs relative to benefits in an effort to avoid true engagement over what people care most about.

The human rights framework is also about institutions. It clarifies the duties and obligations of states, recognizing that the state is an arena of struggle requiring collective action for people to claim rights. The human rights approach is not simply an abstract set of ideas, but is embodied in national and international procedures, structures and institutions. It is not individualistic, although it recognizes the importance of the individual. Instead, the human rights framework links individual substantive freedoms to collective action and collective rights. It democratizes economic policy-making—requiring accountability, participation, and transparency—allowing people to exercise their civil and political rights in support of a more just economy.

Index

Locators in *italics* refer to figures.